LADY ROMEO

◆ ◆

The Radical and
Revolutionary Life of
Charlotte Cushman,
America's First Celebrity

Tana Wojczuk

AVID READER PRESS
New York London Toronto Sydney New Delhi

AVID
READER
PRESS

Avid Reader Press
An Imprint of Simon & Schuster, Inc.
1230 Avenue of the Americas
New York, NY 10020

First Avid Reader Press hardcover edition July 2020

AVID READER PRESS and colophon are
trademarks of Simon & Schuster, Inc.

For information about special discounts for bulk purchases,
please contact Simon & Schuster Special Sales at 1-866-506-1949
or business@simonandschuster.com.

The Simon & Schuster Speakers Bureau can bring authors to
your live event. For more information or to book an event,
contact the Simon & Schuster Speakers Bureau at 1-866-248-3049
or visit our website at www.simonspeakers.com.

Interior design by Lewelin Polanco

Manufactured in the United States of America

1 3 5 7 9 10 8 6 4 2

Library of Congress Cataloging-in-Publication Data has been applied for.

ISBN 978-1-5011-9952-3
ISBN 978-1-5011-9955-4 (ebook)

For my family

Contents

Contents

It is that which is under pressure,
particularly the pressure of concealment,
that explodes into poetry.

—*Adrienne Rich*

LADY
ROMEO

prologue

◆ ◆

The crown was made of pale green laurel, fit for a Caesar, and tied with a white ribbon to symbolize royalty. A handsome young actor carried it onstage on a cushion of purple velvet. Charlotte had chosen a simple dress for the occasion, in a gray silk that matched the steel in her hair. Now in her late fifties, Charlotte had already spent a lifetime being judged by the press, who found her "lantern jaw" ugly but her performances "electrifying." One friend said her mouth was like "the Arc de Triomphe" (it was both a jibe and a compliment). As she greeted the audience, her large, deep-set gray eyes lit up with pleasure.

"She is the rage. Gentlemen reproduce the color of her favorite mulberry morning gown in their scarves and cravats—ladies emulate each other in exactly copying the motion of her hips as she walks the stage," reported the *New York Tribune*, "the press follow her from the first preparatory 'hem!' of her entrance to the final movement of her embroidered handkerchief as she soothes the tragedy-startled rouge upon her cheek."

It was November 1874, and it felt as though all New York City were crowded into Booth's Theatre for Charlotte Cushman's farewell performance. An enormous crystal chandelier presided over the grand room, the beautifully dressed men and women crushed and breathless below. Edwin Booth, who owned the theatre, had hung red, white, and blue drapery in honor of Charlotte, the "American Queen of Tragedy." New York's wealthy, famous, and powerful sat in the box seats, crushed against blue velvet, or leaned, smoking, against Grecian pillars that shone richly with golden gilt. Politicians joined socialites and actors: Governor of New York John Adams Dix; Governor-elect Samuel Tilden; Mayor Havemeyer and his successor, William Wickham, who was negotiating with the French over how much their Statue of Liberty should cost New Yorkers; railroad magnate Cornelius Vanderbilt; and Peter Cooper, inventor of the steam engine and founder of Cooper Union. Above them dangled "clinging vines and branches of artificial grapes."

Standing on the apron of the stage, Charlotte could see thousands of fans crowding excitedly into every available space in the theatre. They stood along the aisles at the back, and in the galleries they leaned precariously over the railings. At a signal from the orchestra the audience turned their faces up to be beatified. Tonight, Booth's Theatre was a place of worship.

Charlotte, however, could see the machinery behind the

marvel. She could see the musicians watching her from the sunken orchestra pit, a new innovation in theatre. Booth's boasted other new technologies, like a sprinkler system to douse overzealous special effects, hydraulic lifts to move scenery, electric spotlights, and forced-air heating.

That night, Charlotte bookended her career by performing the same role she had made her debut in forty years earlier, Lady Macbeth. Throughout her career she had given Shakespeare's characters new life, keeping Shakespeare himself alive when his work could have become a dead thing on the page. She had become famous for her "breeches parts," competing with male actors for men's roles over four decades: Macbeth, Cardinal Wolsey, Henry VIII, Hamlet, and especially Romeo. Though often described as mannish, even "epicene," Charlotte had dazzled fans of every gender as Romeo in her brilliant red-and-turquoise tunics and skintight leggings, with a dagger strapped to her thigh.

A professor from New York College read an ode by Richard Stoddard written in Charlotte's honor. It was called "Salve Regina," translated as "Hail Holy Queen," and modeled on a hymnal of the same name. "Shakespeare!" the poem began, invoking the god of the theatre. "Honor to him and her who stands his grand interpreter. Stepped out of his broad page upon the living stage."

Another speech, this time by American literary critic and poet William Cullen Bryant—white-haired and white-bearded, the elder statesman of arts and letters and the powerful editor of the *New York Evening Post*. To Bryant and the assembled elite of New York society, Charlotte was America's "bright, particular star," and its most profitable commodity. To the working-class audience who'd waited in line for hours to buy tickets, she was "our Charlotte." Everyone was so familiar with Charlotte's work Bryant did not have to list her famous roles by name. Then the Arcadia Club presented Charlotte with a large bouquet of flowers, and Bryant placed the laurel wreath on her head amid a maelstrom of applause. Thus it was that in America in 1874 a fifty-eight-year-old Shakespearean actress was crowned queen.

"I was, by a press of circumstances, thrown at an early age into a profession for which I had received no special education or training," Charlotte explained to the audience. "I had already, though so young, been brought face to face with necessity." She spoke for once in her own words, rather than those of the Bard. "To be thoroughly in *earnest*, intensely in earnest in all my thoughts and in all my actions, whether *in* my profession or *out* of it, became my one single idea," she continued in that unusual voice: warm, woody, and worn to splinters by years of overwork. She paused as the audience applauded. "Art is an absolute mistress; she will not be coquetted with or slighted; she requires the most entire self-devotion, and she repays with grand triumphs." The theatre erupted.

Charlotte left before the applause had died away. She gathered her things, and her maid, Sallie, collected her costume. Then they left the theatre through the back door, at 23rd Street near Fifth Avenue. Edwin Booth and his colleagues had built her a bower of pine branches, sweet and herbaceous, and lithe young actors lit her way with torches. They would likely have carried her on a palanquin, but she was too stout for that. Charlotte climbed into her carriage, and collapsed against Emma with relief. Emma Stebbins had been Charlotte's wife in all but name for more than two decades, even putting her own promising career as a sculptor on hold to take care of Charlotte in her illness. The press referred to Emma as Charlotte's "friend" or "companion," but they called each other by other names. Early in their courtship, Charlotte began calling Emma her Juliet and signing letters "your Romeo." To friends, Charlotte referred to herself as the man of the house. Though she and Emma were not, Charlotte admitted, as passionate as they once were—Charlotte had played Romeo to more than one Juliet since they'd been together—they had made homes in five cities and on several continents. They had survived war, infidelity, and Charlotte's celebrity. Hopefully, they would now survive Charlotte's fans.

Whipped into a frenzy of adulation, the crowd surged against the carriage and almost knocked it over. As the driver urged the horses forward, policemen ran ahead, trying unsuccessfully to untangle the snarled traffic. But more people kept arriving, jamming against streetcars and then pouring out into the road. Charlotte watched in amazement, and amusement, as several men took it upon themselves to unharness the horses from her carriage and pull it slowly through the oceanic crowd.

———

Charlotte was exhausted. For the past decade she had performed through gruesome pain, her body besieged by cancer. Only recently, she'd undergone another painful surgery to remove a tumor from her breast, flabbergasting friends by refusing to be sedated with chloroform. She made this decision after researching her condition in medical journals, some written in German, which explained the dangers of the drug, including cardiac arrest and death. But away from the stage she grew depressed, praying that God "take me quickly at any moment so that I am not allowed to torture those I love by letting them see my pain."

Thankfully, her destination that night wasn't far. Recently completed, the Fifth Avenue Hotel stood at the center of the new theatre district that now radiated from Madison Square Park. Overlooking the park, the massive hotel had been literally built over the bones of the poor, sitting on land that had once been a potter's field and claiming a full city block from 23rd to 24th Street. It was also the unofficial political headquarters for politicians from Tammany Hall.

People with torches lined the carriage route in a long procession. Looking out from inside, Charlotte and Emma tried to guess how large the crowd was; Charlotte thought it was at least twenty-five thousand. When they arrived at the hotel, she was startled to see "rockets set up all the way along up to the front entrance," and as she walked toward the entrance she heard "indescribable noise and confusion." It reminded her of the fireworks she and Emma used to watch in Rome, at the Piazza del Popolo. "The whole big square in front of the Fifth Avenue Hotel was crammed with human beings," she later wrote. "They could not move, they were so densely packed."

Once inside, Charlotte and Emma squeezed along the corridors of the building, which were as crammed with people as the street. From their rooms they could still hear the crowd shouting for Charlotte. Then suddenly amid the noise and confusion a sweet sound rose up. A choir had assembled under their balcony and began to sing. In the heart of the largest, most exciting city in America, Charlotte, who had once had to cover up the fact that she was too poor to pay for her own costume, stood on the balcony and listened to New York serenade her. It was a farewell fit for American royalty.

"What is or can be the record of an actress, however famous?" Charlotte asked in her unfinished memoir. "Other artists—poets, painters, sculptors, musicians, all produce something which lives after them," but not actors. Charlotte knew she would not live forever in the unreliable memories of her fellow Americans, but her legacy continued in the work of her contemporaries. Like many women of her time, her lasting impact could be found in the actions of those she inspired.

From girlhood she was taught that theatre was sinful, yet Charlotte Cushman became an actress and then America's first celebrity. For much of Charlotte's career theatre audiences were mainly men, and women were not allowed to attend the theatre alone. Yet she inspired passionate responses in both men and women. To men, she embodied the man they wanted to be, gallant, passionate, an excellent sword-fighter. To women, she was a romantic, daring figure, their Romeo.

American artists and writers who later became famous were starstruck by her, and she was a household name on two continents. Nathaniel Hawthorne wrote home to his wife, Sophia, to tell her that Charlotte Cushman was staying at his hotel. Walt Whitman was awed by the "towering grandeur of her genius." In 1858 Louisa May Alcott wrote in her diary: "Saw Charlotte

Cushman and had a stage-struck fit." Charlotte's talent even made Alcott wonder whether it was in acting, rather than writing, where her own talent lay. Alcott's relatives, however, were horrified by the idea, and she soon gave it up, working "off my stage fever in a new story." That story was a prototype for her novel *Jo's Boys*, in which a young woman falls in love with an actress based on Charlotte Cushman.

After watching her wring the blood from her hands as Lady Macbeth, President Lincoln walked from the theatre to his desk, where he took up a draft of the Gettysburg Address and wrote about the boys he had sent to their deaths, resolving again "that these dead shall not have died in vain."

Before Charlotte, America had no celebrities; now they manufacture them like blue jeans. She made a lasting impression on young women like Alcott, who saw her as a model of women's independence and a symbol of their "incarnate power."

chapter one

The First Disaster

◆ ◆

I f Charlotte Cushman's life were a play, it would begin like something out of Shakespeare, with nature's rebellion and man's disquiet.

The great experiment of America was only a half century old. Despite American independence, the British still loudly disrespected American sovereignty. America was by many accounts hardly a country at all. "The effect of democracy," wrote Alexis de Tocqueville in *Democracy in America*, first published in 1835, "is not exactly to give men any particular manners, but to prevent them from having manners at all." And if there was one thing American men lacked, it was manners. They drank too much, swore profanely, and spit on the floor. Abroad, America was considered a "vulgar" nation populated by "the dregs of

Europe" and "religious fanatics" who were not educated or aristocratic enough to govern themselves.

In 1812, the new nation had again gone to war when the British began to board American merchant vessels, capturing the ships and conscripting their seamen by force. It took three years, but America won this second war of independence, though it left their capital in ruins.

Outside of the cities, plains of wildflowers, ancient forests of elm, cedar, and pine, canyons and waterfalls made the landscape a natural wonder, but it had not yet produced writers or artists to celebrate its beauty and energy; its future laureate, Ralph Waldo Emerson, was merely a thirteen-year-old boy living in Boston, while twelve-year-old Nathaniel Hawthorne wandered the woods in nearby Salem. The poetry of Walt Whitman and Emily Dickinson still slept underground, waiting for spring. Though the United States was a country populated by American Indians, immigrants, political and religious refugees, speculators, and profiteers—the most diverse intersection of cultures since Cleopatra's Egypt—it was still seen as a land without culture, or as one European traveler put it, a "nation of campers."

But in July of 1816 it was also a nation about to meet its greatest actress. A woman who would insist she was destined for greatness at a time when women did not have careers or own property, were legally enslaved to their husbands if they were married, financially imperiled if they were not, had no public institutions dedicated to their art, scholarship, or health, and could not even go to the theatre alone or linger alone in a public place. At a time when actresses were thought of as little more than prostitutes, one actress would triumph in the most unlikely way.

Charlotte Cushman came from two of the oldest American families. Her mother, Mary Eliza Babbit, was decended from a wealthy family of Harvard-educated men and vivacious women. Her grandmother's impressions could make a table erupt in laughter, and although her grandfather was a lawyer, he rarely charged his clients, spending his free time playing the violin and singing "from dawn to dusk." Charlotte's aunts and uncles were also musical. Uncle Charles had been a beloved local performer in their hometown of Sturbridge, Massachusetts. (He died young.) UncleAugustus, meanwhile, moved to Boston to become a merchant seaman and helped bring professional performing arts to the city when he became a founding investor in the Tremont Theatre. Charlotte's mother, Mary Eliza, was "a good singer, a good scholar" and the most talented dramatic reader in her class.

Mary Eliza was twenty-two when she married Elkanah Cushman, a man nearly her father's age, with a family from a previous marriage. Elkanah had grown up under extreme pressure to succeed, his family the proud but poor descendants of a line of Puritan preachers who could trace their American roots to the *Mayflower*. To them, singing and dancing were sinful—theatre even worse. But Elkanah, the fifth Cushman man to bear the name, broke from his family traditions, leaving home at thirteen and walking on foot from Sturbridge to Boston to seek his fortune. By the time Mary Eliza was introduced to him as a potential husband, Elkanah was forty-four and a successful Boston merchant with his own name over the door.

Mary Eliza Cushman paced the wide floorboards of her

home in Boston, heavy with her first child and growing more uncomfortable and anxious every day. It was 1816, the year of no summer. "The seasons turned backward," one New Englander recalled, and as spring turned, the sky grew mysteriously darker and temperatures dropped. In April, farmers—encouraged by the initially balmy weather—had already sheared their flocks. Then, suddenly, it grew so cold that the ground began to freeze, forcing farmers back into the fields where they tried desperately to tie the wool back on their sheep. Animals died by the thousands. The birds of spring—brilliant goldfinches, ruby-throated hummingbirds in coats of bottle-green, indigo buntings, mockingbirds—froze in the leafless trees, and were dead by the time they hit the ground, songs stopped in their throats. The land was eerily quiet.

In early June, it snowed. A white fur cloak lay gleaming on Boston Common and along the outstretched branches of the Great Elm. In Vermont, farmers tied rags around their crops to keep them from freezing and the poor foraged for "nettles, wild turnips and hedgehogs." The economy of New England was still largely agrarian, and the poor were especially vulnerable to catastrophic climate fluctuations. Thousands starved, thousands more fled to the Midwest.

In the newspapers some argued the crisis was caused by deforestation, while others blamed Benjamin Franklin's lightning-rod experiments. Most believed the intemperate temperatures were caused by either volcanic eruption or brief but powerful eruptions of light and heat from the sun. There was more to the mystery, wrote one journalist, riffing on *Hamlet*, than "our philosophy e'er dreamt on."

Throughout "the poverty year" as many called it, Elkanah Cushman continued to go to work, despite the fact that few of his remaining customers had money to pay. Elkanah was a well-respected businessman, and government contracts helped his business through the crisis. He had weathered rough times before: after raising himself up from poverty, he made a tidy fortune importing goods from Europe and the Indies, and when the British began seizing American merchant ships in 1812 he went to war against them. His first child was conceived six months after peace was declared. On the 4th of July he and his very pregnant wife celebrated the country's fortieth birthday in overcoats and mittens. On July 23 Mary Eliza gave birth to a daughter without anesthetic. They named her after Mary's sister Charlotte.

Charlotte Cushman was a bright, energetic, and healthy child who loved to run fast and climb high. She grew up strong and tall, with a passion for books. Like many American children, she learned three texts by heart: the Bible, the Brothers Grimm, and Shakespeare.

Built around a bustling port, the Boston of her childhood still retained the rough magic of a little town surrounded by big woods. The Cushman family grew, and soon Charlotte was playing in the woods with her younger brother Charles, teaching him how to climb trees and make mischief. "Climbing trees was an absolute passion," she later said. "Nothing pleased me so much as to take refuge in the top of the tallest tree when affairs below waxed troubled or insecure."

Charlotte's experience of America for the first ten years of her life was of an uneasy nation in constant upheaval. The War of 1812 had caused a deep recession, which led to a series

13

of financial crises that businessmen like her father struggled to climb free of. The 1807 ban on international slave trading had a boomerang effect that meant the domestic slave trade exploded. In 1820, the Missouri Compromise enshrined slavery as a permanent condition in the South, allowing Missouri to enter the union as a slave state, while keeping Maine free. Genocide against the Seminoles in Florida and the Cherokee in the West filtered through to Charlotte as adventure stories, and in Byron's odes to Daniel Boone.

Socially, the country was also changing. Charlotte could read the advertisements for British actors' first American tours. The star power of Edmund Kean, William Macready, Fanny Kemble, and Sarah Siddons attracted audiences to theatres in New York and Boston. Unlike her parents, who grew up thinking novels were trashy and lowbrow, Charlotte grew up reading Mary Shelley's *Frankenstein* and Jane Austen's *Emma*, which was published the year she was born.

Raised on a diet of adventure stories, Charlotte began to chafe against the social conventions for how women should look and act. Nice girls did not climb trees, or beat boys at races, or laugh at their own jokes. Charlotte, however, declared herself a "tomboy," and as the oldest of the family she was a tough act to follow. When Charlie was born, he was in effect the second son. She agreed to play dolls with her little sister, but while Susan industriously sewed her dolls new clothes, Charlotte "ruthlessly" cut their heads open "to see what they were thinking." She was no good at sewing, she said, but "could do anything with tools."

It may have come as a surprise to her parents when ten-year-old Charlotte fell in love with her youngest sibling, baby

Augustus. She declared him *her* baby, her "child-brother." She was possessive, bragging that Augustus was "by far the cleverest" of the Cushman children, "keener, more artistic, more impulsive, more generous, more full of genius." He was "my child," she insisted, and he loved her "best in all the world."

Still, as the eldest, Charlotte was "tyrannical" to her siblings, though "very social and a great favorite with the other children," as she later wrote. She made her friends roar with laughter with her "vivid representation of a hen pursued and finally caught, or of the strange, weird, mistrustful behavior of a parrot." She was always curious about what people were thinking, and observed how their mannerisms betrayed psychological secrets. One afternoon Mary Eliza caught her staring at their pastor across the table, mimicking him as he drank his tea. "Charlotte, take your elbows off the table and your chin out of your hands," her mother scolded. "It is not a pretty position for a young lady!" Charlotte obeyed, but felt stifled by the corseted world, and continued to look for outlets for her energy and ambition.

At school, she was not only popular, but a strong and competitive student. She won a medal for arithmetic and kept the title year after year. She also excelled at dramatic reading. Her uncle Augustus saw her talent and encouraged her with prizes. He was often away at sea, but when he came to port he urged Charlotte to cultivate her talent for singing and performance.

Encouraged by her uncle and bursting with creative energy, Charlotte often rallied her siblings and friends to put on plays for the adults. Charlotte wasn't shy about bossing the other kids around, and when she passed out roles she always cast herself as the hero. After reading a play only once she had much of it memorized, and her vision of a character usually came quickly and fully formed. In the evening, the troupe of kids would transform one of the rooms of the house into a theatre, with Charlotte striding across their makeshift stage in pantaloons, a wooden sword strapped around her waist.

Elkanah worked long hours, so Charlotte and her brother Charles often walked from their house in downtown Boston to Long Wharf to visit their father's office and rummage around his warehouse filled with exotic treasures. Long Wharf lay at the heart of the city, the chaotic intersection of India, Commerce, Market, Commercial, and Mercantile streets. As they made their way Charlotte and Charles could hear gulls crying over fish guts and the shouts of the longshoremen, and watch the hunchbacked stevedores loading and unloading cargo from tall-masted ships packed so tightly you could almost walk across.

It's unclear who had the idea first. That day Charlotte and Charles made a new game of jumping from one of the ships to the next. Boston's Long Wharf stretched 1,586 feet into the deep water of the Atlantic with room for nearly fifty ships to dock at one time. Could they get to the end without touching land? They walked up the gangplank to the deck of the first ship. If any of the sailors noticed, they were too busy, or knew them too well, to care. It was exhilarating at first, leaping over the canyon of dark water to land soundly on the next ship, the sharp report of their feet hitting the deck. Then Charlotte leapt but misjudged the distance and fell into the dark water of Boston Harbor.

Filthy water rushed in through her nose and into her mouth. Her heavy petticoats turned to wet rags, then to ballast, and she began to sink. *I'm dying*, she thought, as the waters went over her head.

Then hands plunged into the water and she felt herself being hauled up, waking out of a terrible dream. The sailors dried her as best they could and gave her a spare pair of overalls and a jacket to wear instead of her wet clothes. They led her back to her father's office still shaken, wearing a sailor's rough trousers: a tall, raw-boned girl new-baptized as a man.

Soon after Charlotte's near-death experience, her father disappeared, leaving the family with no visible means of support. Charlotte later called it the "first disaster" of her life. It felt like drowning.

Debt collectors descended on the Cushmans like ants at a picnic. Mary Eliza moved them from one boardinghouse to another, but it was no use. On the day the debt collectors finally caught up with them, Charlotte and Mary Eliza watched the men carry the past away on their backs, hunched over with the weight of family heirlooms.

Mary Eliza finally settled them at 41 Brattle Street, where with few other options for bringing in her own income, she used the little money she had left to open a boardinghouse. At thirteen, Charlotte dropped out of school to work for her mother full-time. (Charles and Susan were too young to help and Augustus was still a toddler.) Mary Eliza could have sent her children to relatives—well-meaning friends in New York even offered to adopt Charlotte—but she refused to break up her family.

Their new neighborhood was a mix of high and low classes.

It was a short walk to the genteel meadow of Boston Common and also around the corner from the Tremont Theatre and the actors, politicians, wealthy men, and prostitutes who frequented it. The actors would become Charlotte's mother's best clients. The Cushmans had gone from being the pedigreed family of a prosperous merchant to genteel poverty. It pained Charlotte to see her brother Augustus growing up without the ease and luxury she'd taken for granted as a little girl. She worked every day for her mother, but although the boarders helped feed and clothe them, Charlotte was determined to lift her family back out of poverty, somehow.

It was no easy task. Window-shopping in the boutiques around Long Wharf and Boston Common, one saw very few women working. The shop clerks, the carriage drivers, the lamplighters, street sweepers, and newspaper sellers were men. Sometimes Charlotte might see lady's maids in sere cotton dresses like her own, appearing briefly in the doorway of some stately home to dump out their masters' chamber pots, or occasionally through the back curtain of a haberdashery, a woman surrounded by heaps of fabric, bent double as she made tiny stitches along a man's pant cuff. Education made little difference; even women who had finished high school had no universities that would admit them. Charlotte lived in a half world, denied even the physical freedom of riding out on her horse alone. She could have looked for a wealthy husband, but was scornful of women who believed marriage would bring them independence; it was, she would later write, a form of sexual slavery. She wanted more than that.

Charlotte's work was grueling. She emptied chamber pots

and stripped beds, washed endless piles of linens, their sodden coils heavy as a body. She dusted the dressers and lamps and tables with a goose wing. Several times a day she filled the ash bucket and dumped hot ash down the toilet to muffle the smell. If the weather was nice, she opened the windows and lifted the sash to bring sweet air in and let the bad air out. Every few months, they washed down the bedposts with lye to kill the lice. But it was here the first glimmer of an idea came to her. Her eyes burning from lye as she scrubbed the kitchen floor or with her hands plunged into a basin of soapy dishwater, she listened to the actors and actresses. They might complain about late payments, drunken costars, costumes rubbed raw, and nervous exhaustion from train travel, but they also recited lines from great poets and playwrights, told good jokes, read widely, traveled constantly, and told stories about stars who were invited to dine with royalty and made great fortunes.

The next time Uncle Augustus came to visit them in Boston, Charlotte pleaded with him to take her to a play at the Tremont Theatre. She knew she was her uncle's favorite and that he felt sorry for her. Though Augustus and Mary Eliza's family may have once had money, there was none left to help Charlotte or her siblings. Augustus had always believed in Charlotte's intellect, and now here she was changing guests' stained sheets instead of coming home breathless and excited after school. When the newspapers announced that the famous British actor William Charles Macready was coming to Boston, part of his first American tour, it was too good a chance to miss. He agreed to take Charlotte to see Macready at the Tremont in Shakespeare's *Coriolanus*.

chapter two

Quest

———————◆ ◆———————

If her father had not left, Charlotte would have been forbidden to enter a theatre. In the 1800s audiences were primarily men, and theatres catered to male audiences by offering liquor and bawdy afterpieces that ran late into the night. In "that dark, horrible, guilty 'third tier'" of all the large theatres men could purchase sex with prostitutes. Actresses were often former prostitutes and were considered only a step above your common whore. To become a star, an actress had to retain some veneer of respectability, and making it was a matter of survival as much as talent. Some older actors bragged about preying on the superlatives, or "supes," who played minor roles like chambermaids and dancing girls. Girls who rose to fame on their good looks quickly found themselves wrung out and replaced, and yet the rare actress like the great British tragedian Sarah Siddons, who rose to fame, was treated like a queen. America had produced no actresses to rival Siddons, in part because no respectable family would allow their daughter to go onstage. It was seductive, however. Stepping into the theatre, you entered a raucous, debauched space, but it also promised connection with European high-culture through opera, Greek tragedy, and most of all Shakespeare.

The theatre wars in America went as far back as the Puritans who tore down Shakespeare's Globe. Puritan polemicist William Prynne, born around the time the Bard was writing *Hamlet*, warned that "theater breeds spiritual anarchy by encouraging such inversions of nature as transvestism, irreverence and hypocrisy." He argued that watching plays with "whores and strumpets" onstage would lead to "if not actuall, yet contemplative adultery." Early American settlers feared the theatre in part because it was in competition with the church.

Nathaniel Hawthorne, growing up in puritanical Salem, Massachusetts, understood the Salem witch trials as a form of high drama themselves: mass hysteria and public murder of so-called witches by Puritans, the spectacle of young girls forced to confess to bizarre sex acts. As the future mayor of Salem Charles W. Upham wrote in 1831, "Pastors, deacons, church members, doctors of divinity, college professors, officers of state, crowded, day after day, to behold feats which have never been surpassed on the boards of any theatre." Like Upham, Hawthorne did not "doubt the power of imagination so much as he fear[ed] it."

Even before the American Constitution had been ratified, Americans were debating what to do about the theatre.

Most plays were written by British writers, "that heathen riter Shakespur" the most popular among them. During Charlotte's childhood, Shakespeare was performed in American theatres at least as frequently as in England, but a uniquely American theatre had not yet been born. Americans might have gained the right to call themselves a country, but culturally, they were still a colony. One problem, according to Herman Melville and others in the Young America movement, was that Shakespeare continued to overshadow American genius. Possibly more problematic was the enduring puritan squeamishness about theatre in general.

In the years following the Revolutionary War, Americans had turned their attention to the culture and entertainment their new freedom could afford them. Puritans saw clearly that theatre was in competition with the church for butts in seats. Other anti-theatre factions argued that since most plays were British, theatre was a form of cultural imperialism. (Ironically, theatre bans throughout the revolutionary period only solidified the British monopoly on theatrical culture.)

It seemed that every American had an opinion on the theatre paradox. On one hand, Americans were free people who believed that the government should not be allowed to dictate their entertainment choices. In Boston, one senator even argued that theatre was "the natural right of every man." Yet the majority of the wealthy, influential Americans who made the laws mistrusted "every man," and doubted that the average American had the intellectual capacity to know what entertainments were good for them. These same would-be aristocrats hired actors for private performances to entertain family and friends.

Foremen argued that the theatre would entice the poor to waste money and the working man to shirk his duties. But workers protested when their theatres were closed down. The Clergy recognized that the theatre was a powerful force that shaped public morals, but they failed to imagine working-class audiences could have any other response to a play than to emulate it. Clergymen "assumed the actors must be depraved because those who represented a passion had internalized it" and predicted that "women would expect to be treated like goddesses after viewing a play, causing the family to fall apart."

But, by the early nineteenth century it had become clear that, like prostitution (which it was often likened to) theatre was nearly impossible to regulate. Laws banning it were unenforceable and only undermined the authority of the fledgling legal system. American writers pleaded for more theatres to be opened, so they could have an outlet for their plays. By the time Charlotte was born, the debate was no longer about whether theatre should exist in America, but about how Americans could use the theatre to develop their own culture. Still, the America of Charlotte's youth was a country whose vision of itself had yet to come into focus.

When Charlotte and her uncle Augustus arrived at the Tremont Theatre the sun was dipping low in the late afternoon, casting long shadows across the cobblestone street. The theatre's marble facade shone creamy white. Men leaned against a low stone wall, hands in pockets, hats tipped low to block the sun. Young boys dirtied their fine clothes playing tug-of-war with stray dogs, and women with parasols wore bonnets and long pastel dresses held away from their bodies with stiff crinolines and bustles, looking like bells about to be rung.

They were all here to see the great British actor William Charles Macready. As a boy, Macready grew up in his father's London theatre. He was a pretty child and his father cast him in the girls' parts. Young Macready did well in school, and dreamed of leaving the theatre to become a lawyer. He had finally started law studies at Oxford, when his father's theatre went bankrupt and his father was locked up in debtors prison. Rather than let the theatre fail, Macready dropped out of Oxford and returned home, where he took over as manager and stepped into his father's leading roles. He excelled at tragedy and soon became a star. Now, he was the most famous actor in England. With no telephones or telegraph, indeed with no electricity at all, news traveled very slowly. It spoke to Macready's fame that even before he boarded the steamer in London, every city in America knew he was coming.

Though he belonged to a suspect social class, Macready's celebrity won him invitations to dine alongside the wealthiest and most respectable families in England—and their patronage had helped make him rich. In London, he was close friends with Charles Dickens, with whom he shared the experience of rising from penniless youth to fame and fortune. He was also prone to the kind of attention-grabbing tantrums that made news. Once, when a costar's death throes threatened to upstage him, Macready broke off mid-sentence to hiss that the upstart should "die further off."

Inside the Tremont, Charlotte sank down into a plush velvet seat. The mixing scents of sawdust, varnish, shoe polish, hair oil, lavender water, and under it all, filtering through layers of damp, summer-weight wool and broadcloth, the yeasty, dirty-penny smell of sweat and excitement filled the air. Hundreds of bodies waited for the curtain to rise. Then Macready took the stage. He was handsome in his Roman armor, and his short tunic showed off his long legs. He had a mane of thick, dark hair; expressive, wide-set eyes; and full, sensitive lips. His Coriolanus "seemed a man of quick, irritable feelings, whose pride was rather galled than wounded," both "the Coriolanus of Shakespeare and of nature."

Coriolanus was a strange choice for an American audience. The play is unabashedly anti-democratic. The Roman general Coriolanus returns from battle and his fame ensures him a place in the Senate. Not-so-secretly, however, he despises the populace, comparing them to a ravenous belly and a many-headed monster. Shakespeare seems to go out of his way to demonstrate that the rabble are ill-suited to governing themselves. Written at the turn of the fifteenth century, it was the same criticism Americans still had to stomach from their former rulers in England.

But if the audience suspected anti-Americanism at the heart of Macready's performance, they were too overawed to say so.

Leaning over the railing of her uncle's box seats Charlotte could see families in the pit unwrapping a dinner of dark bread and cheese, apples, a whole roast bird pulled from a hamper and torn limb from limb. The women's gallery was a murmur of silk, the self-satisfied sheen of beaver pelt, the glow of red fox, green cloth dresses, fashion-forward paisley silk from France. The ladies glinted in constellations, the gaslight refracting off their jewelry in the dark like stars.

Charlotte was impressed by Macready, but not so over-whelmed she couldn't begin to see how it was done. Like him, she was drawn to heroic characters, but there were few of these written for women. To be a successful actress you ought to be beautiful. Charlotte knew she was not a beauty like the British acting legend Sarah Siddons or her niece, Fanny Kemble, a rising star. Still, she longed to perform. Opera had a better reputation than theatre and so she determined to become a professional singer.

She had reason to hope. Everyone who heard Charlotte's voice said it was remarkable. Where most singers labored to per-fect one range, Charlotte could sing in nearly a full two registers. She could sing soprano parts, stretching her vocal cords long and thin to reach the highest notes, and she had a deep, textured, res-onating "chest voice" that could reach some of the deepest notes. She could also sing contralto, the lowest range for a woman—so rare that most opera companies cast these roles with male castrati.

Charlotte had been singing in the choir at the Unitarian church, where her pastor was a brilliant young scholar named Ralph Waldo Emerson. Emerson was born in Boston as the son of a preacher. He entered Harvard at fourteen and when he grad-uated he entered the ministry. Emerson's ministry allowed him to sketch out a radical philosophy that elevated the individual's spiritual path above the hierarchies of the church. When Char-lotte met Emerson he was newly married, and besotted with his nineteen-year-old wife, Ellen. When Ellen died suddenly of tu-berculosis, Emerson was distraught and found that his faith gave him little comfort. Ultimately, he discovered he could not bring himself to give the sacrament in good faith and left the church forever.

Whether or not Emerson's radical philosophy shaped Charlotte's own, she shared his uniquely American belief that the path toward God could be charted by the individual. American Unitarians believed that one must exercise reason in interpreting the Bible. Strict interpretations of the Bible that held, for example, that Jesus's reincarnation was real were hard to accept for more scientifically minded parishioners. But Charlotte, like Emerson, took this philosophy a step further, believing that if you cultivated your own moral character, then your own intuition would lead you down the right path. Young and ambitious, there was tremendous spiritual and intellectual energy coiled inside her and it seemed like the more she spent, the more she had.

Anxiety, too, drove her. In the four years since her father left, Charlotte had gone from being the protected eldest daughter of an upper-class family to a striving, working-class woman. Fear of artistic failure coupled with her sense of moral obligation to her family. If Charlotte could prove that she could support them, she could claim the right to be independent. Ironically, however, the price of that freedom was that all her creative energy had to be directed toward one goal: success.

In 1833 the famous, glamorous singer Mary Ann Wood arrived in Boston. She checked in to the Tremont House, a high-class residential hotel near the Tremont Theatre. Wood was in town to perform in Mozart's comic opera *The Marriage of Figaro*, and she and Charlotte rehearsed at the same studio.

Wood was exactly who sixteen-year-old Charlotte dreamed of becoming: a world-famous opera singer with a trunk full of beautiful costumes, a woman who had parlayed her talent into fame and a successful artistic career. Wood also had taken the radical step of suing her first husband—successfully—for divorce in her native Scotland, and was now remarried with a young child. It was nearly impossible for a woman to get a divorce, and the very subject was taboo. And yet the divorce had not hurt her career. In fact, Wood had earned a fortune singing throughout Europe, a fortune she hoped to increase on her first American tour. She traveled with her husband, Joseph Wood, also a singer. When they reached a new city, they cast their supporting roles with local performers. When Wood said she was looking for a female singer to accompany her someone suggested Charlotte and she invited her to audition. It was the kind of opportunity that could turn a former choir girl into a star.

Charlotte began to prepare for her audition with Mrs. Wood, propelled not only by the promise of fame but by the determination to save her family from ruin. It was a difficult task. She had never been to a theatre outside Boston, had never heard Rossini's *Cinderella* in Paris, or felt the heat from the oil lamps illuminating the cavernous La Scala in Milan. She was thoroughly unlike the glamorous divas, with their pulchritude and their jewels. Assessing her looks, Charlotte stated frankly, "I am not beautiful." Talent would have to carry her, but her talent was still raw and untested. She had never even performed outside of church.

With her family's fate hanging over her, Charlotte arrived at the Tremont boardinghouse and nervously found Mrs. Wood's room. When she knocked, Wood opened the door wearing her usual fine silk gown, her luxuriant black hair cascading in tendrils over her shoulders. The difference was stark. Charlotte was tall and raw-boned, and wore her hair parted in the middle and looped over her ears, an old-fashioned style that emphasized her wide-set eyes and heavy, square jaw.

Throughout Charlotte's audition Mrs. Wood was quiet, her delicate oval face inscrutable. After the last, soaring note died away, she simply got up and left the room. Charlotte waited uncomfortably in the elegant parlor until Wood returned with her husband, Joseph. Mrs. Wood asked if Charlotte would sing the song again.

Charlotte sang again. When she finished, both Mr. and Mrs. Wood jumped to their feet, clapping ecstatically. They assured her she had done very well and, as Charlotte later told her mother, "that such a voice, properly cultivated would lead me to any height of fortune I coveted."

On the evening of the show, Charlotte performed for Boston's elite as well as her family and friends. The show was a success, and newspapers raved not just about Mrs. Wood but Miss Cushman, the local girl whose voice would surely make her a star.

But just as important as Charlotte's talent was her innate ability to draw people in. She was warm, enthusiastic, and a devilishly hard worker. Wood admired her and they became friends, though Charlotte developed an unrequited, Labrador-like crush that lasted long after Wood left Boston. Before she left, however, Wood introduced Charlotte to a local manager and singing coach named James Maeder. Maeder, too, saw Charlotte's potential as a singer and invited her to study with him. When she explained that she couldn't pay, Maeder and his wife agreed to let Charlotte work off her lessons in trade as their maid.

James Maeder's wife was the somewhat notorious Clara Fischer Maeder. Clara was a diva, a former child star who boasted that she had been acting since the age of six. She had played Richard III—hilariously, in a fake mustache—at twelve. Clara had made a fortune in her youth, but her extravagant tastes meant that the Maeders, with all their airs, were often broke.

Charlotte trained with Mr. Maeder and cleaned his house for three years. Finally, in late 1835, when she was nineteen, he cast her in a supporting role alongside his wife in Mozart's comic opera *The Marriage of Figaro*. Though she was naturally a contralto, she sang soprano as the Countess Almaviva, a role at the very peak and precipice of her natural range. She did well at first, and when Mr. and Mrs. Maeder decided to bring *The Marriage of Figaro* to New Orleans, where the couple had theatrical connections, they asked Charlotte to come with them. She had never traveled outside of New England and never left her mother's side. But she was ready.

chapter three

Transformation

◆ ◆

The water of the Mississippi was a thick, dark cloak sweeping solemnly aside as the steamship moved inexorably south. On board, Charlotte could feel the river hurrying them forward, and her thoughts raced even faster. She filled the many long, boring hours reading the kinds of books that might fill in the gaps in her education, which had ended at thirteen. Charlotte had never been out of New England and did not want to seem uncultured. New Orleans was said to be more European than American, a mixture of French, Spanish, and British influences. It seemed both thrilling and terrifying. Some called it "the City of Gomorrah" or "Southern Babylon" because prostitution was tolerated and because the Port of New Orleans was a key point in the southern slave trade.

As they came closer, Charlotte saw a few buildings protected from the river by a levee, a high embankment, without which, noted the travel writer Frances Trollope, "the dwellings would speedily disappear." Then around a bend in the river rose New Orleans. Dripping with vines and Spanish moss, repeatedly soaked by rains that swept through it and strove to rot buildings as quickly as they could be built, the city was in a constant state of entropy. Energy in, energy out. Build. Destroy. Build again. Transformation was the rule.

Charlotte disembarked at the Port of New Orleans in December 1835, exhausted and nauseous, and found a boardinghouse near the St. James theatre where she would be working. New Orleans was a study in contrasts. Near the St. James was the fashionable Esplanade Avenue: women dressed in "*la mode Parisienne*," in plaid dresses, and men in top hats, checked trousers, and coats cut away at the front to show their shapely legs. A few streets over was one of many large slave markets, where plantation foremen came to buy the men, women, and children slavers had captured from Africa.

It was head-spinning. Charlotte left her luggage at the boardinghouse and walked to the St. Charles Theatre for rehearsal. In the front of the theatre was a large marble staircase from which to gaze at the statues of Apollo and the Muses, flanked by Grecian pillars. A giant stone eagle perched above the entrance. But actors were not allowed to be in the "front of house," so Charlotte went around to the rear, passing a coffin factory before she found the back door. Inside the ceiling soared. She was confronted by the four-thousand-seat auditorium, the largest outside of Milan. The theatre's owner, James Caldwell, also owned the city gasworks, and he'd made the St. Charles an impressive advertisement for the power of gas. The walls and ceiling were brightly painted, covered in frescoes and gilt. From the center of the ceiling hung a glittering thirty-foot-wide chandelier, hung with twenty-three thousand dazzling crystal gems, lit by gas jets. The seats were draped in red, blue, and yellow silk. Caldwell had built the theatre for his young wife, a beautiful actress, spending more than $350,000—more than it cost to build the first White House.

On opening night, Charlotte sang *The Marriage of Figaro* at the highest part of her natural range. She struggled to fill the cavernous space, and soon she realized, with horror, her voice was failing her. The sophisticated New Orleans audience was merciless, and the critics savaged her the next day for the fact that she was nineteen and inexperienced. "The worst Countess we have had the honor of seeing," one critic wrote. "Miss Cushman can sing nothing," declared another. The kindest said she was merely "bearable." The show was canceled after three performances.

But Charlotte had signed a contract and was bound to a certain number of performances. So she continued humiliating herself onstage night after night in other supporting roles. She had worked for three years with Mr. Maeder to achieve the clear, elastic tone of an opera singer, and it was suddenly gone. Her tone was now "aspirated," roughened, and "woody." Though tragic for an opera singer, the loss paradoxically also added something new. One friend said Charlotte's tone was now like "the expression of wilful passion suppressed."

Then, a few months later, in early 1836, a deus ex machina. Charlotte received an urgent summons to theatre owner James

Caldwell's office. Caldwell's wife had died suddenly, and he was struggling to find someone to fill in for her at short notice. Although he was grieving his wife, the performance was a benefit for the theatre manager, William Burton, and Caldwell did not want to cancel. He asked if Charlotte would act in his wife's place. She would fulfill her contract and have Caldwell and Burton's gratitude. She agreed immediately, even though the part was one of the most famous and famously difficult roles for any actress: Lady Macbeth.

"Never fell in love with a lord, never made an immense fortune, and never played Lady Macbeth," wrote one of Charlotte's contemporaries. It was a role actresses dreamed of, and one typically reserved for a star.

The role was intimidating in part because it was so closely associated with the legendary British actress Sarah Siddons. Siddons was first cast in the role in 1785, a little more than fifty years earlier. At the time she was unfamiliar with *Macbeth*, and stayed up late reading the play by candlelight: "I went on with tolerable composure in the silence of the night (a night I can never forget)," Siddons wrote in her memoirs, "till I came to the assassination scene," where Macbeth botches the murder of the king. To keep herself and her husband from being caught, Lady Macbeth must wrest the bloody daggers from his hands. As Siddons read, the play began to scare her so badly she had to put it down. She grabbed her candle and "hurried out of the room in a paroxysm of terror," imagining that her own silk dress rustling

Sarah Siddons as Lady Macbeth (1797)

behind her as she climbed the stairs was a ghost following her. It would be another six years before she agreed to play Lady Macbeth again, but she would eventually make it her signature role.

Slim and statuesque with large, dark eyes, Siddons was a celebrated beauty. And her feminine figure and seeming fragility aided her in getting the audience's sympathy in tragic roles. Lady Macbeth, who brags about being steely enough to kill her own child, is one of the most unsympathetic women in theatre, but Siddons found a way around this. She decided her Lady Macbeth should be "fair, feminine, nay, perhaps even fragile."

Siddons dressed herself for the part in bridal white, with a nun-like white wimple that framed her guilt-stricken face. Her Lady Macbeth was a woman who used her beauty to seduce Macbeth into doing what she wanted.

Siddons had died in 1831, five years earlier, but thanks to a recent biography she was more on the audience's mind than ever. Nostalgia elevated the great tragedienne still higher, and Charlotte seemed to be competing with a ghost.

Physically, Charlotte could not have been more different from Sarah Siddons. At five-foot-seven she was a towering figure onstage, taller than most men. Her body was strong, and she moved like a "pythoness." Far from fragile, Charlotte had what one rival called a "lantern jaw," wide shoulders, and large breasts and hips—erotic, perhaps, but not traditionally feminine. She had to find a new way to play Lady Macbeth, and quickly.

With only a few days to learn the part, Charlotte rose early each morning and walked to the theatre, where she rehearsed for several hours with James Caldwell. At night she climbed up to the garret of the house where she boarded and sat on the floor reading the lines out loud to herself until she had them memorized.

She enjoyed the process of rehearsal, which could be surprisingly funny. The actors wore their everyday clothes to rehearsal, and she could watch an actor pacing around the stage in his overcoat, carrying an umbrella as he dripped water everywhere, reciting Shakespeare as though talking about the weather. Or an actress wearing clothes several seasons out of date, practicing her pirouettes while nearby "a couple of begrimed men in shirt-sleeves and smelling of tar and things are kneeling on the floor hammering away at the gas arrangements or something about the scenery." Charlotte had a good sense of humor, and her jokes and delight in the absurd quickly made her a favorite among her fellow actors.

Because they always rehearsed in street clothes, Charlotte was able to hide the fact that she had no costume for Lady Macbeth until opening day. All the actors were expected to supply their own wardrobe, but she lived paycheck to paycheck, sending

Charlotte Cushman as Lady Macbeth (1855)

home anything extra, and didn't have the money to buy new clothes. As a novice, she also didn't have a closet of costumes to pull from. Afraid she'd be fired, Charlotte waited until the very last moment to tell Caldwell. Alarmed, he quickly dashed off a letter and sent her running to an address he had hastily scribbled on an envelope. Charlotte hurried through the humid streets of New Orleans to the French Quarter and found the address. The celebrated French actress Madame Closel opened the door and both women burst out laughing. Charlotte was tall, thin, and lanky, while Mme. Closel was short, fat, and four-foot-ten-inches tall, with a waist twice the size of Charlotte's and a very large bust. Mme. Closel was good-natured and empathized with Charlotte, so she got to work. She took a seam-ripper to one of her skirts and made an underskirt, taking in another dress "in every direction" to make a queen's costume. "So it was," Charlotte wrote, "I essayed for the first time the part of Lady Macbeth."

The modern technology of the St. Charles helped Charlotte appear more natural than she might otherwise. Most theatres, like the Tremont in Boston, were lit by oil lamps set along the foot of the stage. The lamplight tended to converge on one central spot, leaving the rest of the stage in gloomy semidarkness. Actors had to play all their major speeches from the same place and exaggerate their mannerisms and expressions so they could be seen. Gaslight allowed Charlotte a freer range of movement and expression. For some, the effect was too much. One friend of James Maeder complained in a letter that Charlotte "was almost insane on the subject of display and effect . . . and altogether too demonstrative," "commanding" rather than soliciting the audience's attention.

But the critics agreed on one thing: like Hamlet thrusting his sword through a shadow in the curtains, Miss Cushman had hit immediately on a starring role. "She made the people understand the character that Shakespeare drew," wrote one critic. "She was neither stilted, nor mock-heroic, nor monotonous, but so fiercely, so vividly natural that the spectators were afraid of her as they would have been of a pantheress let loose. It was impossible New Orleans should long retain such a woman."

Finally completing the terms of her contract, and with her first wages in her pocket, Charlotte decided not to follow the Maeders back to Boston. James Barton was so impressed by her talent and work ethic that he wrote her a letter of introduction to a theatre manager named Thomas Hamblin in New York.

Two years earlier, in 1834, Hamblin had taken over and rebranded the failing Bowery Theatre as "the people's theatre." He took advantage of nativist, anti-British, sometimes anti-abolitionist sentiment among the white American working class in New York. Unlike the nearby Park Theatre, Hamblin's theatre advertised to working-class audiences, and he was looking for new American talent. But his unpredictability, drinking, and reputation for violence made it difficult to keep that talent for very long. His source of actresses tended to be the underage prostitutes who were his mistresses. Under Hamblin's management, the Bowery had earned the nickname "the Slaughterhouse," for Hamblin's fondness for bloody melodrama.

But Charlotte didn't let any of these warnings stop her. In the fall of 1836 she boarded a steamboat aptly named *The Star* in the Port of New Orleans. It would sail up the Mississippi

River to Philadelphia, where passengers could catch a train on one of the newly opened railway lines to New York. The steam engine fired up with an immense bellow, belching smoke, and Charlotte began moving slowly northward, against the current.

chapter four

The Star of the Bowery

──────── ◆ ◆ ────────

T rain travel was deafening. At each stop from Philadelphia to New York Charlotte heard bells ringing,
porters bawling out instructions, and passengers
shouting at one another over the noise until finally
the doors slammed and, with a "tremendous pop as of a colossal
champagne-cork," the machine started up again. Traveling this
way was still a novelty, and not a pleasant one. Even compared to
traveling in a coach with four horses, the train went so fast that
the towns between Philadelphia and New York became unreal,
"like pictures on the wall." Outside the window flowers by the
side of the road became "streaks of red or white," while fields of
grain became "great shocks of yellow hair" and "fields of alfalfa,
long green tresses." Charlotte found the experience both exciting

and tedious. It was so enervating and exhausting that many travelers had to recover under a doctor's care. *The Lancet* reported a new study on "train-induced fatigue." The boredom of train travel, wrote the French novelist Gustave Flaubert, made one want to "howl like a dog."

The train finally let Charlotte off in New Jersey, at the Pennsylvania Railroad Station, and she paid the fare for the ferry to Lower Manhattan. New York was experiencing a summer heat wave, but the wind across the river was cool. Charlotte stood on the deck as the boat churned through the river water. She was always a bit seasick on boats and the fresh air calmed her stomach. The island of Manhattan stretched out along the Hudson River from the green cuff of Battery Park peeking out from the weft of dense buildings, to the north where the buildings petered out into farmland and marshland around 28th Street, and the forested area near Harlem, which was close enough for a weekend ramble and a picnic.

Charlotte disembarked from the ferry and began walking through Lower Manhattan. She searched for a cab to take her to her boardinghouse in the stifling humidity and heat, wearing a boned corset and several layers of petticoats, unable to avoid the smell of rotting garbage and unwashed bodies. It was not exactly glamorous. Around her she could hear a babel of languages and accents: Polish, Russian, German, Chinese, Yiddish, Spanish, French, rhyming Cockney, Irish brogue. The architecture, too, spoke a thousand dialects. The financial district had its elegant marble facades, its streets populated by men in dark suits with worried expressions. St. Paul's Chapel, where George Washington had prayed, and the Washington House, where he prepared for battle, and the elegant Park Theatre on Chatham Row with its rhythmic arches and columns. Continuing up Chatham Street, one found the ostentatious Bowery Theatre with its screaming eagle over the door, covered in gold gilt, looking to one overheated observer "as if he could clutch almost anything in his talons, from Indian babies to Mexican candlesticks." The eagle was part of Hamblin's plan to whip up the audience's patriotism "till they feel a comfortable assurance that every American can 'whip his weight in wild cats.'"

As the cab's horse picked its way slowly through the streets, stopped every few feet by someone dashing across the road, Charlotte saw a curious thing. Amid the crowded buildings there was a great empty space, like a row of missing teeth. Her cabby knew this neighborhood well. It was called the Burned District.

Where one of the greatest financial centers in the world once stood was now a charred mass stretching seventeen blocks from Beaver Street to Water Street in Lower Manhattan. Less than a year earlier, on the freezing night of December 16, 1835, the Bowery had blazed like a world in hell. Copper roofs poured down themselves in great molten drops, iron doors buckled, clapboard houses were quickly swallowed by fire. An icy wind blew snow and ash into the faces of onlookers and forced back the merchants trying to save some of the goods from their stores. One person remembered the smell of coffee being burned and looking down to see fine lace trampled into the snow. Temperatures were so low the rivers froze, stranding ships in the harbor, and water moved through the firefighters' pumps in a slow trickle of icy sludge. Ships moved to the middle of the East River for safety from the blaze, only to find hours later that they were frozen in midstream.

By the time it was over, the fire had destroyed most of the financial district. Banks, stores, and the Merchants' Exchange were wiped out, sparking a financial crisis that still reverberated months later. Yet, as Charlotte was now discovering, everything in New York—even destruction—was a spectacle. A guidebook to New York City published the year Charlotte arrived included the Burned District as a tourist attraction. If you had the money, you could buy a pair of gum arabic shoes "as wide as they were long" and hire someone to lead you on a walking tour through the mud—a slurry of animal feces, ash, human waste, and industrial garbage—that stood six inches deep in the streets.

Thomas Hamblin, like his contemporary P. T. Barnum, understood the attraction of spectacle. He specialized in "blood-and-guts" melodrama and used dangerous special effects like gunpowder and real fire to excite the audience. Although Charlotte's manager in New Orleans had written her a letter of introduction to Hamblin, she wrote first to Edmund Simpson, the man in charge of the Park Theatre. The Park was the most prestigious theatre in New York. Compared most often to London's Royal Theatre on Drury Lane, it catered to New York's elite. But Simpson's response disappointed her. She would need to audition first, and even then he could not guarantee her a job. She was offended. After her success as Lady Macbeth in New Orleans, it was hard for Charlotte to imagine making her New York debut in anything but a starring role.

Only then did Charlotte write to Hamblin. When she arrived in his office, he was impressed, even more so when she showed him her reviews. He told her she was exactly what he was looking for at the Bowery, a woman of hurricane-force passions who would not be dwarfed by his elaborate sets, special effects, or by himself. Six and a half feet tall, Hamblin had a "horror of little women" as he put it, and appreciated Charlotte's height. She would look good next to him onstage. With thick, curling dark hair and a square, dimpled chin, Thomas Hamblin was a lady-killer. (Two of his wives actually died under mysterious circumstances.) His alcoholism and violent temper meant that actors rarely stayed with him very long, but he had still pulled the Bowery out of bankruptcy. He was less interested in Charlotte as a romantic conquest than as a unique attraction for his audience.

"If a philosopher wishes to observe the ultimate product of civilization, and has strong nerves, and senses not over-delicate, he may do well to take a seat in the pit of the Bowery," wrote one contemporary observer. Fights broke out frequently, and the audience even sometimes climbed onstage to intervene in stage battles if they thought it wasn't a fair fight. From the stage, an actor could see "apple-munching urchins" and women in the pit nursing babies and men on the infamous "third tier" having sex with prostitutes. Hamblin had drilled peepholes for police to watch the spectacle from a private room. He made his special effects greater and greater to capture the audience's attention, using so much gunpowder in one battle scene the audience had to run to the windows and throw them open to breathe. Once when an actor playing a king pretended to fall asleep, some of the audience got onstage and took turns trying on his crown.

Despite their troublemaking, the Bowery audience was engaged in the show and passionate about Shakespeare. It was the best school a young actress could get. When the Gallery Gods in the top tier got bored, for example, the actors knew it. They "amused themselves by throwing pennies and silver pieces on the stage, which occasioned an immense scramble among the boys" who jumped onstage to gather up the coins. A serious flub might occasion "a rain of vegetable glory."

"Throw not the pearl of Shakespeare's wit before the swine of the Bowery pit," went one popular saying. And yet it was the working-class Bowery audience that kept Shakespeare on the stage in New York night after night. The slums in which the Bowery "b'hoys" and "g'hals" lived were densely populated, dangerous, and crowded with half-starving children. Abandoned by parents too poor, infirm, or addicted to care for them, some of the children who survived formed themselves into gangs with names like "the Dead Rabbits." The theatre was their one amusement. Though many were illiterate, they knew most of Shakespeare by heart.

William Shakespeare intentionally wrote for both working-class and wealthy audiences. His heroes are often royalty made powerless in some way. His villains are frequently comic, turning aside to share a bawdy joke with the audience. Shakespeare had to be a master equivocator to survive in paranoid Elizabethan England, where a playwright could be "racked" and tortured for seeming to support the wrong political or religious party. Rather than pick sides, his plays move fluently between spectacle, drama, and poetry, between high and low culture.

"Theatre is divided into three and sometimes four classes," explained Charlotte's friend, the actor Joseph Jefferson. Each class of people had different ideas for what made a great night of entertainment, and the actor's challenge was to appeal to them all. Jefferson's solution was to act as broadly as possible. In his eyes, each "suggestion should be unmistakable; it should be hurled at the whole audience, and reach with unerring aim the boys in the gallery and the statesmen in the stalls." It was an artificial style that flattened the characters until they seemed like shadows flickering on a screen. As audiences tired of this style, special effects became all-important. But many longed to be swept up in the drama, to feel with the character and see their own lives reflected even in the kings and queens onstage.

After a very brief period of rehearsal Charlotte prepared to make her New York debut as Lady Macbeth opposite Hamblin's Macbeth. But just before opening night she fell dangerously ill with rheumatic fever. She lay in bed shivering, then burning, in excruciating pain. Rheumatic fever, wrote one contemporary physician, "licks the joints, but bites the heart." On September 12, still weak and feverish, she was finally able to take the stage.

The Bowery audience immediately embraced Charlotte as one of their own. As she performed, they burst out in spontaneous applause, interrupting her speeches. She understood the character and made Lady Macbeth seem horribly real. Although one critic complained "she had no charmes of person, for she was ugly beyond average ugliness"—he admitted her "homely" face could come alive with a light that was "transcendently beautiful." Her "ungraceful form" could "quiver with a passion that was electrical," and her "wiry voice" became "tremulously sweet," as though intoxicated by love, and then "gutturally savage with the demoniac rage of intense, venomous hatred." Rare for American actors, it was said that Charlotte enunciated beautifully and with sensible line readings showed she had carefully studied the part. She was declared "the star of the Bowery."

On her first day off, a week later, Charlotte took a coach to Harlem and went for a long walk in the woods. By the time she got home, however, her fever and chills had returned. She could not act for weeks. While convalescing, Charlotte left her costumes at the theatre, feeling they were not yet hers since Hamblin had paid for them. But while Charlotte was at home recovering, one of Hamblin's special effects went out of control. The Bowery Theatre caught fire and burned to the ground. The sets, props, and all of Charlotte's costumes were inside. With no theatre to run, Hamblin canceled all the actors' contracts. The timing couldn't have been worse. Charlotte's mother, Mary Eliza, had just sold the boardinghouse and come to live with her in New York. At twenty years old, Charlotte prepared to start over—for the third time.

chapter five

American Genius

* *

You must exercise your Genius in some
form that is essential to life.

—*Ralph Waldo Emerson*

L ooking at her mother's face in profile as she gazed
at the Hudson River out the train window, Charlotte could see a grim set to her mouth, the worry
lines in her brow even at rest. She was devoted to her
mother; "after some important event," wrote a friend, "[Char-
lotte] could not rest till she had written her mother about it."
Her brother Charlie was working as a sales clerk in New York,
and Susan was staying with relatives. So it was Mary Eliza and
young Augustus who would be joining Charlotte in Albany.
Augustus would go to school nearby in Greenbush while

Charlotte worked. It was a sacrifice for everyone, but she was convinced it would be worth it.

By now, she believed that acting was her divine path. As her former pastor Mr. Emerson put it, "to create is the proof of a Divine presence . . . whoever creates is God."

"God helped me in my art-isolation," she later wrote. Even her father's disappearance had pushed her toward this goal. "If I had been spared this early trial," she wrote to a friend, "I should never have been so earnest and faithful in my art . . . given my entire *self* to my work." While most women her age were having children, she determined to be married to her art. What she did want was to keep working so she could give her family some financial security and her little brother a new life.

Augustus sat next to her on the train. For him, travel was still a novelty. She loved having him close, and had found him a good school just across the river from Albany. Charlotte looked forward to the day when Augustus would surpass her. She believed he was the cleverest in the family and, though born into greater poverty than she, "keener, more artistic, more impulsive, more full of genius."

Greenbush Classical School was a small boarding school for the sons of New York's elite. Many of Augustus's future classmates were the children of New York state senators who worked across the river. The ancient pine forests the area was named after rose up around it, deep green and intoxicating. Charlotte, who loved horses, admired the wide open meadows.

After getting Augustus settled, Charlotte and Mary Eliza continued on to the capitol. Crossing the Hudson River, they traveled along one of a series of roads that radiated from the center of Albany like a star, or like the wheel of fate. It was called a turnpike, named after the spiked wheel medieval kings placed across roads to defend against enemies or extort tolls from their people. The theatres here drew large crowds of many races, made up of the merchants who brought goods to and from the largest port on the Eastern Seaboard and to ships bound west along the newly completed Erie Canal—which connected the Hudson River at Albany with Lake Erie.

Charlotte performed almost nightly in starring roles. She and Mary Eliza lived in a hotel occupied by members of the state senate and house of representatives, and they soon discovered that one of the outgoing representatives was Mary Eliza's cousin. The connection helped them gain the trust and patronage of the wealthy and powerful politicians who ran the city. The joke was that "more of the members of both houses could be found at [Charlotte's] performances than at the capitol."

In the mail one morning Charlotte received an invitation to the extravagant "fireman's ball," an annual dance and benefit that was also an opportunity to mingle. Making an impression there, she knew, could help her career, but it had to be the right one. On the night of the event she spent several hours getting ready, adding a surprising final touch to her usual simple silk dress. On top of her head she pinned an "immense bird of paradise," with eye-catching orange-and-purple plumage. With her height, heeled shoes, and the bird on her head she towered above her companions.

Theatre folk knew how to camouflage flaws. For example, men concealed bandy legs under layers of padded stockings to create the illusion of fullness, while women dyed their hair or wore prosthetic bosoms. But instead of minimizing her oddities, Charlotte exaggerated what many considered her defects.

The effect was mixed. Men and women disagreed about her appearance; to many men she was simply ugly, a "bull in black silk," while women tended to admire the way she embodied both masculine and feminine. One female critic described her face as "harsh, but harmonious as Beethoven's chords and discords." It pained Charlotte to be judged by her appearance, but she refused to hide and at the fireman's ball she danced all evening. The local newspaper reported that, at the ball, Charlotte was "magnificently attired . . . she was the observed of all observers, the bright particular star of the evening."

Fame can be fickle, but Charlotte had a canny sense of occasion, and knew how to use it to appeal to her audiences' emotions. At one of her benefit performances, an evening where she would receive all the proceeds from ticket sales, she made the occasion about "Albanians" rather than herself. Before the performance, she found out the names of all the firemen in the city, including the name of every foreman and engineer and of every fire engine. After the benefit, she read a poem she'd composed in honor of the firemen. The literary critic for *Ladies Companion* magazine praised her writing, marveling that she had managed to fit in every name "without injuring the harmony of the verse."

Charlotte's fame grew, and her performances at the Pearl Street Theatre attracted Albany's most fashionable crowd. She began to get offers to perform with famous actors. In October 1836, the legendary Junius Brutus Booth came to town and asked for her to be his Lady Macbeth. Charlotte had grown up hearing Booth's name; when she was celebrating her first birthday, he was publishing the first volume of his memoirs. Booth was British, but America was his adopted home. He had abandoned his first wife, a flower-seller, in England, and had now had several children out of wedlock. Though bedeviled by alcoholism (a lifelong affliction he had passed on to sons John Wilkes and Edwin), Booth was a brilliant actor. Still slim in middle age, he had a handsome, tragic face. The production of *Macbeth* was a success, and Charlotte held her own alongside one of the most experienced actors in the world.

By the winter of 1836 Charlotte was so busy she struggled to keep up with her family's lives, and she missed Augustus. She paid for his school, room, and board but rarely got to see him. Her typical day included morning rehearsal, evening performance, and dinner with friends—which now included some of the powerful Albanians who regularly came to her shows. Usually getting home around midnight, she stayed up later studying lines, sometimes with just a few hours to learn a new role before rehearsal the next day.

Rehearsals are an actor's school, and Charlotte always tried to excel, but the process was still new to her. She was confronted every day with the theatre's foreign language, a maze of new words—downstage (toward the front), upstage (toward the back), stage left (the audience's right), stage right (the audience's left), carmine (rouge), scrim (a thin screen at the back of the stage), cork (burnt cork to darken the actor's skin), and a hundred others—that allowed the actors, craftsmen, and stage-hands to communicate quickly and efficiently. It was like being on Long Wharf again, listening to sailors speaking of keels and crosswinds.

She also had to learn to manage her salary and negotiate her own contracts. An inexperienced actor could find her salary whittled away by fines if she wasn't careful. If she stayed too long getting her makeup on in the green room and missed her cue, she would be fined, and fined again for coming late to rehearsal or failing to be "off book" (having her lines memorized) along with the actors around her. Charlotte was confronted every day by the fact that she knew far less than the other actors and had to work doubly hard to prove herself. It made her long for Augustus, who always made her feel secure and at home. In the few hours she had to herself, she responded to Augustus's adoring, ardent letters.

"My Dear Darling Sister," Augustus wrote to her on February 19, 1837, "I am sending you a (play)bill for an exhibition we are going to have next Friday evening." He clearly missed her, too. Still, he was making friends. At eleven years old, Augustus took after Charlotte in his personality. He was funny, intelligent, and friendly. Though Charlotte's moods and health sometimes suffered from overwork, Augustus was healthy and happy. Charlotte longed to have him by her side, but she hoped the separation would be short-lived. Though normally exceptionally careful with money, she bought Augustus a lavish gift. She took some of her earnings and went to the horse-trader to pick out a horse for him. Then she went to the tailors and ordered him a little riding jacket, cut out of bright blue wool. He could go riding as soon as the weather warmed.

Springtime was dreary, with cold rain and frost still hard in the ground, but Charlotte was feeling optimistic. She had almost made enough money to take Augustus out of school and move the whole family back to New York. There, she hoped to try again at the prestigious Park Theatre.

One day in early April 1837, Charlotte heard someone knocking at her door and was surprised to find a messenger holding a telegram. She opened it, and read with horror that Augustus was dead. "The ground liquified under me," she would later write. "I felt the waters go over my soul." Her horror deepened when she learned he had died after falling from the horse she had so lovingly picked out for him.

After Augustus's death, Charlotte fell into a deep depression. Although mentally and physically exhausted she had to continue performing almost nightly despite her grief. It was a distraction, but her heart was no longer in it. The vision that kept her ambition alive was of her family together again, safe and happy as they had been before her father left. But she felt she'd failed to keep Augustus safe, and she blamed herself for giving him the very instrument of his death.

In her misery she asked God what kind of sign this was meant to be. Should she give up or push on through her grief? The answer came in the form it nearly always did—an emergency that pressed her into service.

Susan Cushman, Charlotte's sister, had been living with half siblings who seemed to pay little attention to her, their needy relation. Susan was fifteen—pretty and penniless. She soon caught the eye of Nelson Merriman, a man more than fifty years older than her. Though Susan did not encourage him, Merriman wrote to Mary Eliza suggesting that he adopt Susan as his daughter so she could inherit his fortune when he died. When Mary Eliza refused, he proposed marriage to Susan instead. "I am on my deathbed," he swore, claiming he only wanted to be Susan's benefactor. Finally, Mary Eliza agreed, believing she was securing her daughter's future. Charlotte, who was busy preparing to debut her Romeo, was too distracted to realize the significance of her mother's decision, and merely expressed her disgust that Mary Eliza would allow Susan to marry someone she did not love. What she didn't know was that Merriman was also a fraud.

A few weeks later, Charlotte and her mother packed their things and returned to Manhattan. Work would be a welcome distraction from grief, but Charlotte still mourned, remembering the child-brother she once rocked in her lap. Packed in her suitcase was Augustus's last letter and his little blue riding jacket. She would bring these with her wherever she went.

chapter six

Gypsy Queen

———— ♦ ♦ ————

L abor saved me," Charlotte later wrote to a friend about the weeks following Augustus's death. She did not want to be crushed by grief, so she conquered it by working herself into exhaustion. Her plan was to "suffer *bodily* to cure my heart-bleed," to "strew ashes over the loss of my child-brother." So she took a job where she knew she could flagellate herself with "all the mortifications in my profession": the Park Theatre.

When she first returned to New York City in May of 1837, Charlotte went to work at the National Theatre in New York as a "walking lady," taking any part they would give her. But she also wrote to Edmund Simpson, the manager of the Park Theatre, hoping to get a contract there. Meanwhile, the National put her to work immediately in *Guy Mannering*, a musical adaptation of Sir Walter Scott's novel. *Guy Mannering* is an adventure story that follows a band of gypsies and their queen, Meg Merrilies. Meg adopts an orphaned boy who is secretly a nobleman's son and raises him lovingly as her own. When the boy grows to be a man, his true identity is revealed and bandits immediately kidnap him for ransom. Meg ultimately sacrifices her own life to save her boy. Charlotte was cast not in a starring role but as a "singing gypsy." A comedown from her triumphs as Lady Macbeth and Romeo, but she wasn't in Albany anymore. "Albanians" had appreciated her talent but the goodwill she'd earned there had a poor exchange rate. She would have to prove herself all over again.

She had to be satisfied with small roles, for now. But she was in the center of American theatre, a paid actor with a contract at a good theatre. It was spring. The dogwoods were blooming, and the city was shaking itself off and putting forth new life.

Then, in early May 1837, nearly twenty banks failed. The financial crisis put stress on the theatres, who relied on audiences' disposable income to survive. Edmund Simpson and the co-owner of the Park, Stephen Price, needed something new to lure audiences into their shows and keep them coming back.

One morning Charlotte got word that the actress playing Meg Merrilies was sick and she would need to fill in from her manager at the National that very night. Meg was a leading role, with many lines, and Charlotte had less than a day to learn them. She raced to the theatre to pick up a copy of the full script. Managers normally only gave a full copy of the play to the leading actors, limiting the number of manuscripts in circulation to keep them from being sold to a competing theatre.

But Charlotte had already had her eye on the starring role. When she wasn't onstage singing and dancing in ridiculous musical numbers, she had been hiding in the wings, listening for clues to Meg's character, and noticing where the lead actress— Mrs. Chippendale—made mistakes. Mrs. Chippendale, a British actress, interpreted Scott's Gypsy queen as a young woman. But Charlotte had realized that if Meg had raised a baby boy from infancy into manhood, she would not be young. In fact, since Meg was not the boy's biological mother, she *could* be very old.

Charlotte went to rehearsal the day of her debut as Meg still hoping to "catch some inspiration." Unlike many actors in a starring role, she didn't pay attention to just her own character, but also to how other characters talked about her. Rehearsing onstage with her script in hand, she heard one gypsy say to another that Meg "rules the tribe" and yet "she doates," meaning that she is too tender and maternal. Off to one side, Charlotte took notes, but kept her plan a secret.

That night, when the order for "places" was given, Charlotte did not come to the stage. She was still in her dressing room. John Braham, a "sweet-voiced" young English tenor who was meant to play opposite Charlotte, waited anxiously in the wings for his new costar. Then behind him in the darkness he heard a sound, and when he turned what he saw gave him a cold chill.

From the velvet gloom a thing of supernatural power came forward. The face was deeply carved with dry creek beds of wrinkles, her dark hair, parted in the middle, escaped in uncombed tangles down her back. Her tattered dress was simple and dark, reaching to the floor. The sleeves were cut short to reveal well-muscled arms. She seemed to glide when she walked, like an apparition. In her hand was a tall staff of power, forked at the end. Braham gasped, then realized with a shock that this crone was Charlotte Cushman.

Charlotte had likely taken some of her inspiration from one of her favorite poets, John Keats. Keats's ballad "Meg Merrilies" imagines the character as an emblem of romantic wildness, not beautiful in the traditional sense, but in the way that craggy hills are beautiful. She weaves garlands of woodbine, crooning eerily to herself. Old Meg is "tall as Amazon" but copies womanhood with a tin ear: her cloak is an old red blanket, and she wears a "chip hat," out of fashion for nearly fifty years. Like Lady Macbeth, her power is not quite human.

Moments before the curtain went up, Charlotte crept into the gypsy tent that had been placed for her onstage. Her gray-clad figure seemed to hover, ghostly in the silver moonlight. When the show began and she finally spoke, her voice sounded as if it came from another world, hoarse and broken.

In her next scene she leapt from the wings onto the stage with a "strange, silent spring," terrifying the audience. Then she stood suddenly straight "like a great, withered tree," with her arms outstretched and a "look of fire," as she began to prophesy: "The dark shall be light / And the wrong made right"

"If ever the dead come back among the living," Meg crooned, "I'll be seen in the glen many a-night after these crazed bones are whitened in the mouldering grave." A mere month after Augustus's death the image of bones moldering in a grave was not an abstraction for Charlotte. Spilled blood never dried, "it crie[d] night and day" from the deepest dungeon "to the blue arch of heaven."

At the play's climax Meg and a band of her Gypsy followers

stormed the prison where her adopted son, Harry, was held captive. One of the guards raised his pistol and aimed a shot at Meg, fatally wounding her. Charlotte, one critic recalled, came "staggering" down the stage, with a shriek "so wild and piercing, so full of agony . . . [it] told the whole story of her love and her revenge." When Meg and her followers finally broke through and rescued Harry, she collapsed and died at his feet. A total silence fell over the theatre as Charlotte's limp body was carried offstage. As much as she had terrified her audience, she now made them weep.

The audience saw no more of Charlotte until her curtain call. When she came out to take a bow, her face was bare, and she had combed out her hair, pinned it neatly, and changed out of Meg's soot-stained rags. The effect was electric. It emphasized how different the twenty-year-old actress was from Meg, and made her performance seem even more impressive.

Charlotte Cushman as Meg Merrilies in Guy Mannering

Charlotte had also added an essential bit of spectacle to the show. After Meg died, Charlotte had the rest of the cast sing a little "finale" which gave her more time to rush backstage, wipe off Meg's "wild weird, intense face," and return a sweet, pleasant young woman.

As with Lady Macbeth, Meg seemed to vindicate the widespread fear that female ambition would inevitably tilt into madness. "The Meg Merrilies of Miss Cushman," wrote one critic, "seems to abstract and embody in itself—in a perfect individual reality—all we have seen or known or had presented to us in the stage or closet—of wild women—crazed prophetess—strange in attire—sore distraught in spirit—and borne above the common flight of their sex by something demoniac and supernatural." Charlotte was careful to put distance between the actress and the "wild woman" she portrayed.

When it was all over, Charlotte returned to her dressing room. She was just getting ready to leave when she heard a knock and her costar Braham's voice calling her. Charlotte wondered what she had done wrong, but Braham hadn't come to scold her—he was staggered. How, he asked, did such a young actress learn to do something like that?

She could not explain. For Charlotte, a character was not only learned but grasped at once in a flash of intuition. Then she would distill the character through repetition. Charlotte's Meg was so popular the show was extended. When her stockings wore out, Charlotte mended them rather than buy new ones, to keep up the appearance of age and poverty. When her entire costume needed to be replaced, she dyed the new one by hand, rubbing it with dirt and other mixtures she invented herself to age it. She continued to do her makeup and hair as she had done that first night. For a time, a young painter came to watch Charlotte get ready, to study how she did her makeup. "How," the artist asked incredulously, "do you know where to put in those shadows and lines which so accurately give the effect of age?" But Charlotte only replied cryptically that she put them where she felt they should be.

When onstage, Charlotte disappeared into her character. "Unless one does," she wrote to a friend, "he can never be an actor." When Walt Whitman, the young critic and editor of the *Brooklyn Eagle*, came to see her Meg Merrilies, he was impressed by Charlotte's empathy: "She seems to identify herself so completely with the character she is playing," he wrote, "she loses, for the nonce, every attribute, except those which enter into the making up of what she is to pourtray." (Still suffering from guilt over her brother's death, losing herself was what she had in mind.)

The critical response was overwhelmingly good. Reviewers raved about Charlotte's "virile energy," "pythonic inspiration," and her "noble frenzy of eccentric genius." Her Meg had truly frightened and moved them, and for cynical New Yorkers, this was rare.

Charlotte's success at the National finally helped her secure a contract with the Park Theatre. Once, she had been offended if anyone offered her less than a supporting role. But now, with her pregnant sister and mother to support, she happily signed a contract with the Park as another "walking lady." She would be extremely busy, which was a good thing since she still hoped work would defang her grief. It was not fasting and praying, but it was close enough. She signed on for three years, at $20 a week.

Edmund Simpson, Charlotte's new boss, had managed the Park Theatre for more than twenty years and was an important figure in New York culture and politics. He had hair that curled up from his brow, a wide forehead, full lips, and an aquiline nose. Simpson had been an actor but taken up managing when a tragic accident in the theatre during a performance of *Doctor Faustus* left him partly paralyzed. His business partner, Stephen Price, was a lawyer and son of a powerful New York businessman.

Simpson and Price had made the Park successful, and they could be ruthless to the competition. For example, when the African Grove—the city's only theatre owned and operated by African-American actors—began to compete with the Park's own minstrel shows (which featured white actors in blackface), Price leveraged his family's political connections to get the Grove shut down.

Charlotte began acting at the Park in the sweltering heat of late summer 1837. She took up the grueling schedule of an ensemble actor, playing several different minor roles every week. At home, Mary Eliza helped her sew new costumes, learn lines, made sure she ate, and helped her recover from frequent illnesses brought on by stress. But she could not rest. A new disaster had quickly taken the last one's place. Susan arrived in New York, pregnant and in despair. Merriman had abandoned her as soon as she became pregnant, and after he left she discovered he was not the wealthy man he'd claimed to be. On March 4, 1838, Susan gave birth to a son, Charles Edwin, whom they nicknamed "Ned." Two weeks later, Susan celebrated her sixteenth birthday.

Married at fourteen, a single mother at sixteen, Susan would likely have been forced into prostitution if Charlotte hadn't been able to support the family with her acting. But with a new baby in the family, money was tight. Susan was young and beautiful and Charlotte had the idea that she could go onstage to play opposite her in the more feminine parts. When Ned was old enough to be left with Mary Eliza, Charlotte suggested Susan try a career on the stage. And if hard work had helped Charlotte recover from the blow of Augustus's death, why shouldn't it help Susan recover from her "disastrous" marriage? Their brother Charles was now supporting himself as a salesclerk and this was a rare opportunity for Susan to work, too, so she agreed to try.

Unknown to Charlotte, encouraging her sister to join her at the Park Theatre made her an enemy. Park Benjamin was an influential theatre critic whose mistress was a pretty young actress at the Park named Miss Clarendon. Benjamin was extremely handsome, described as looking exactly like Lord Byron, whom he copied in manner and dress. He was also lame in both legs, and walked "with difficulty on two canes." Susan was now in direct competition with Benjamin's girlfriend, and Miss Clarendon already disliked Charlotte for trying to give her unsolicited acting advice. Charlotte claimed she was being helpful, but Miss Clarendon "ridiculed [me] for my pains."

Benjamin began by mocking Charlotte's performances in the press. Then he wrote to her personally and promised to have her hissed out of the theatre if Susan didn't leave the Park. Far from feeling intimidated, however, Charlotte wrote back immediately. The letter's rhetoric was flawless. She instantly grasped that Benjamin saw himself as a cavalier defending his lady-love, and managed to flatter his ego by taking his chivalry seriously while challenging the assumption that she was any less vulnerable to attack than Miss Clarendon: "I have felt what it is to be defenseless," she wrote to Benjamin, "and would not attack so unfortunate a young lady—but with due deference to you I do not consider her defenseless while she has a person willing to draw a band around him intending to crush one lady upon the ruin of whose reputation that of the young person might be built." Regarding being hissed from the stage, Charlotte completely changed tack, treating this as a strictly business matter rather than a personal threat. Getting a large group together to intimidate her was "a matter requiring some time and trouble" and it would likely only hurt his own reputation. "I think," she concluded, "you have business of more importance." Perhaps calculating the cost versus the benefit of his attack, or feeling he had made enough of a show to please Miss Clarendon, Benjamin backed down, allowing Charlotte to get on with her work. But as she would soon discover, she still had enemies at the Park.

chapter seven

Descent into Five Points

hen Susan opened the paper, she gasped. She
called Mary Eliza over and pointed out the
announcement. "Charlotte will be furious,"
she said. It was February 1839. Frost made
paisley patterns on the windowpanes, and outside horses struggled to pull cabs down the street in deep snow. Charlotte had
not gone to the theatre that day, staying home in front of the fire
with Susan, Mary Eliza, and little Ned, now almost two years
old. But the news Susan brought her was chilling: it was a cast list
for the Park's next production, Charles Dickens's *Oliver Twist*,
with Charlotte in the role of the prostitute Nancy. It was not a
starring role. Charlotte's friend Annie Brewster recalled it was
"always given to actresses of little or no position in the company."

It was also dangerous, since actresses already had to fight against the stereotype that they were essentially prostitutes themselves.

Charlotte was furious, but she couldn't do anything about it. Her contract explicitly said that she had to take any part they gave her. Charlotte suspected that Stephen Price, one of her managers, disliked her. "I was at the mercy of the man," she later recalled. "It was mid-winter; my bread had to be earned. I dared not refuse, nor even remonstrate, for I knew he wished to provoke me to break my engagement."

By casting her as a prostitute, Price was being reckless with her reputation. Playing a prostitute put her in the line of fire for moralizing journalists like Horace Greeley, editor of the *New York Herald Tribune*. Greenley wrote in one review that "a large proportion of those connected with the Stage are libertines and courtezans."

In their New York apartment Susan tried to hush Ned's crying, Mary Eliza mended costumes, and Charlotte sat in a chair reading and rereading Dickens's play. It was clear she could not simply button herself into the role of Nancy as it was already made; she would have to take a seam-ripper to the thing and piece it out herself. She was determined to get the better of her enemy. "What he designed for my mortification should be my triumph," she wrote to Annie Brewster.

Up to the night appointed for *Oliver Twist* she was not seen by anyone except at business hours. She took her meals in her room and spent her time there or out of the house on clandestine rambles. Charlotte was rehearsing in secret, "studying that bare skeleton of a part; clothing it with flesh, giving it life and interest." To really get a sense of Nancy as a human being, and the conditions she had to endure, Charlotte even ventured into Five Points.

Five Points was a place both mythical and material. It was a neighborhood in Lower Manhattan that ran from Bowery to Centre Street, south of Canal Street, where gangs with names like the Forty Thieves and the Bowery Boys battled nightly. Five Points was an inner-city slum; the people there were largely new immigrants from Italy, Germany, and Ireland. Thousands of women who arrived in New York unaccompanied or who had families to support spent short, brutal lives there as prostitutes. Sewage from the nearby canal poisoned the water and the ground, and airless tenements housed sometimes dozens of men, women, and children in one room. Along the canal stood a prison known as the Tombs.

In the eighteenth century, however, Five Points had been the site of a beautiful clear lake called "the collect pond." Nearby Bunker Hill emerged out of miles of forest there, and from its crest you could see birds rippling the waters of the lake: egrets, woodpeckers, black-eyed blue jays, and cardinals in their showy red cloaks. A winding horse path led to small homes, and beyond that the white walls of mercantile buildings, all dwarfed by the spire of St. Paul's Chapel.

Then, around the lake grew a row of slaughterhouses and tanneries, which began to fill the Collect Pond with their offal. By the time Charlotte walked into Five Points in 1839 it was America's first slum. When Charles Dickens visited the neighborhood

Collect Pond, New York *(1798)*

on his American tour, he found it at least as bad as the London slums he fictionalized in *Oliver Twist*: "narrow ways diverging to the left and right, and reeking every where with dirt and filth." Seeing pigs in the streets, Dickens asked, "Do they ever wonder why their masters walk upright in lieu of going on all fours?" The aristocrats of Five Points, it was said, were the butchers, because their children never went hungry.

Middle-class tourists might pay to go "slumming" in Five Points with a police escort, holding camphor-soaked handkerchiefs to their noses to see how the poor really lived, but women rarely went there unless they were dedicated social reformers. A woman did not wander off there alone, without telling anyone where she was going.

Walking alone among the smell of roasted corn and the cries of the "hot corn girls," Charlotte heard music spilling out onto the street from nearly every bar and public house, and a new kind of percussive dancing born in Five Points called "tap." When she got thirsty, she could buy a lemonade or shandy from a German street vendor. Passing a dilapidated building called "the old Brewery" that housed more than a thousand people (once a cheerful yellow, it now squatted in the neighborhood like a toad), Charlotte walked the same streets Whitman frequented. While even well-meaning social reformers tended to think of violence and crime as the special talent of the poor, Whitman saw Five Points as a wellspring of "the Republic's most needed asset, the wealth of stout poor men who will work." Immigrants did their best to make tenement apartments into homes, decorating their mantels with pictures and keepsakes of the life they'd left behind. Although Charlotte's family had come to America on the *Mayflower*, she was driven by the same dream as these new immigrants.

She was empathetic toward the prostitutes she met, and she watched them carefully to find the spark of recognition that would help her bring Nancy to life. She had no trouble finding prostitutes, since, as one observer wrote, "every house was a brothel" and "every brothel a hell." Charlotte also saw generational poverty, and how the lack of opportunities for work was especially crushing for women and girls. It was not unusual, wrote one journalist, for a mother and two or three daughters "to receive their 'men' at the same time in the same room."

As with the character of Meg, the authenticity of Nancy's costume could help her feel real to the audience. During one of her walks, Charlotte offered to trade clothes with a dying prosti-tute. She gave up a simple but well-made silk dress and put on the woman's rags. These would be Nancy's clothes.

The grass around the Park Theatre was crisscrossed with short-cuts. Street vendors sold hunks of gingerbread, oysters, fried beefsteak, and pungent pickled red herring scooped from a bar-rel. Behind the theatre, Charlotte carefully navigated an alley knee-deep with filth. In the bag slung over her arm were a dead woman's clothes. Like the heroine of the Brothers Grimm's "Al-lerleirauh," she'd traded her fine dress for rags, and it had been a fair trade.

In the green room, Charlotte's fellow actors made strange sounds and movements as they warmed up their voices and did calisthenics. She warmed up and dressed in secret. Waiting in the wings for her cue, she could hear the audience laughing and gasping as Dickens's drama unfolded. The warmth of the gaslight dried their wet woolen winter clothes. The theatre was full, from the plush, velvet-lined box seats to the benches where women spread out their wide, rigid skirts. The galleries were draped in a swath of baize, the bright kelly green of a billiard table. Behind the galleries the walls were brilliantly whitewashed and the iron columns that supported them were made to look as though "cov-ered with burnished gold."

Of the three main theatres in New York the Park was the only one considered fashionable, though some secretly thought the Bowery was more beautiful. The third competitor, the Chatham

Theatre, was out of favor, "so utterly condemned by *bon ton*, that it require[d] some courage to decide upon going there." But even in the audience at the Park men stripped off their coats and hung them over the gallery railing, showed up with unshaven upper lips stained by tobacco. The European travel writer Frances Trollope found the audience at the Park "more than usually revolting." The Park had its own infamous "third tier," and almost half of the city's brothels were located within three blocks of the prestigious theatre. To succeed, Charlotte would need to appeal both to high and low, aristocrats and working-class audiences.

Oliver Twist was a story that reminded readers of *Guy Mannering*: a young boy abandoned to criminals who is saved by a woman who sacrifices everything for him. The prostitute Nancy is torn between loyalty to her lover, who is in thrall to the criminal Fagin, and her strong desire to save the orphaned Oliver. Charlotte immediately grasped Nancy's struggle between good and evil, something that resonated with her audience as many found themselves torn between the lures and snares of the city and their own moral compass. Many in the audience did not yet know Nancy's fate. Dickens's novel *Oliver Twist* had been released in serial form, and the final installment had only recently been published in America.

Toward the end of the play, Nancy betrays her lover, Bill Sikes, by freeing Oliver from captivity. When the crime boss discovers what she's done, he orders Sikes to kill her. In her final scene, Nancy is in bed. Hearing a noise, she sits up suddenly. She is not alone. A shape in the doorway moves toward her, but with relief she realizes it is only Sikes. She reaches for him, but he roughly pushes her away and blows the candle out, ordering her to get up. Nancy pushes herself off the bed. "Is that you, Bill?" she asks. "Oh I'm so glad! But you've put out the candle." Bill Sikes snarls at her, "There's light enough for what I've got to do." Nancy pleads with him, then tries to scream. Sikes strikes her in the face with his pistol.

In other productions Sikes dragged Nancy away to murder her offstage. But Charlotte had a better idea. She choreographed a "fearful struggle" between Nancy and Sikes, which her height and strength made into a real contest. She gave the audience a chance to believe Nancy might actually get away. This was true to Dickens's novel, which described the murder in gruesome detail.

"The 'murder of Nancy' was the great scene," enthused one critic. Charlotte instructed the actor playing Sikes to drag Nancy around the stage by her hair, while looking defiantly at the gallery. The audience hissed him, cursing "like a Handel Festival chorus." Sikes dragged Nancy around the stage twice more. He shook his fist at the audience "like Ajax, defying the lighting." The crowd's roars grew louder and more blasphemous, the noise and excitement rising to a climax Charlotte had carefully orchestrated: "Sikes, working up to a well rehearsed climax, smeared Nancy with red-ochre, and taking her by the hair (a most powerful wig) seemed to dash her brains out on the stage, no explosion of dynamite invented by the modern anarchist, no language ever dreamt of in Bedlam could equal the outburst."

The audience mourned and screamed foul play, so totally caught up in empathy for the poor murdered woman they seemed to forget entirely that she was a prostitute, the likes of whom died on the streets or in the Tombs prison in Five Points every night. Charlotte, drawing inspiration from her five days in Five Points and from Dickens's novel, had done the inconceivable and made Nancy into a martyr.

Once again, Charlotte had taken a supporting role and made it into theatrical gold. Tickets sold out and critics raved. One critic, Walt Whitman, argued that Charlotte's performance was proof that America was at last ready to compete with Europe as a cultural powerhouse. Whitman was part of a growing group of American writers calling for more recognition by their countrymen—they included Ralph Waldo Emerson, Henry David Thoreau, Bronson Alcott, Orestes Brownson, and other members of the "Transcendental Club." The club's first meeting had been titled "American Genius: the causes which hinder its growth and give us no first-rate productions."

Whitman was one of many watching Charlotte's career in the hopes that she would finally prove that Americans could produce more than pale imitations of European art. When he saw Nancy, he found her delightfully appalling, writing in his column for the *Brooklyn Eagle* that it was "the most intense acting ever felt on the park boards." He believed that no one who watched her could help but "marvel at the towering grandeur of her genius." He was convinced that audiences would now stop flocking to see "fifth-rate artistic trash" from Europe.

Simpson and Price, however, seemed immune to Charlotte's charms. When her contract expired after three years, she asked for a raise, but they turned her down. Furious, Charlotte quit.

She spent a year as the manager of the Walnut Theatre in Philadelphia. Then William Macready arrived in New York and asked her to come act with him, but the problem was that she had a contract with the Walnut she could not get out of. She made a plan. She said yes to Macready and took the train back and forth from Philadelphia to New York, acting different parts every other night. It was grueling, but she hoped that Macready's seal of approval would help her gain recognition.

Macready was the British star she had seen on her first visit to the theatre as a young girl. His star power meant he could essentially set his own schedule, decide what plays he wanted to do and whom he wanted to work with, and demand a cut of ticket sales. Charlotte wanted all that for herself.

She and Macready became friends, and she confided her ambitions to him. His advice was simple: save your money and go to London as quickly as you can. Her talent would never be appreciated by American audiences until she succeeded in Europe. As proof, he pointed to the American actor Edwin Forrest. Forrest had done well in London and this made him a star at home. (In fact Forrest's London success was due in part to critics paid to "puff" the show—giving it good reviews—and audiences stocked with his friends.) Macready disliked Forrest, whom he found coarse. If Forrest could do it, Charlotte could, too. Unlike Forrest, she had taken elocution lessons so she could do dialects and hide her American accent. Her careful line readings and intellectual understanding of Shakespeare also gave her an advantage over most American actors.

Macready convinced her, and Charlotte decided to follow his advice. She was still paying for her family's room and board but began putting away some money in secret to go to London.

chapter eight

First Love

———— ◆ ◆ ————

Macready had convinced Charlotte that London was the only place to advance her career. Americans followed where European culture led them, and they would not take Charlotte into their hearts until she had conquered England. In any case, 1844 was an election year, which would have made it even harder to capture newspapers' attention stateside. Both instinct and good sense told her to go to London, but she delayed actually leaving because she had fallen in love.

Rosalie Sully was the daughter of the famous American portrait artist Thomas Sully. His fluid, soft, idealized portraits of the rich and famous, and especially women and children, were extremely popular. Sully had nine children and supported his late brother's children on the income he received as an artist. Rose and Charlotte met after she commissioned Mr. Sully to do her portrait. It took longer than expected because Charlotte was difficult to capture in a still image. Sully threw out his first painting of her, convinced it didn't do her justice.

Rose also wanted to be a painter, and she, too, began working on a portrait of Charlotte—a miniature. Sully encouraged his daughter's career and had made a portrait of her holding a portfolio full of paper and a pencil, her hat on a bit askew, ready to journey into the hills to sketch. In another portrait by her father, Rose peers like a satyr over her sister Blanche's shoulder, her dark ringlets bouncing merrily, smiling gleefully as she meets the viewer's gaze.

Since meeting Rose in the fall of 1843 through a mutual friend, Charlotte had spent every weekend at her house, equally enamored of Rose and her large, close-knit family. The chaotic Sully house delighted her with the noise and children and the electric glimmer of Thomas Sully's famous clients. Whenever she arrived at the house, she raced eagerly to visit Rose in her own art studio, to sit and read while Rose painted or walk or ride with her through the countryside. To Rose's family Charlotte was an entertaining, if somewhat eccentric, new friend: she went walking with Rose's oldest sister and mother and came regularly to dine, where she would give command performances of Shakespeare's monologues, sing, and recite poetry. But behind Rose's closed studio doors Charlotte became Romeo begging for a kiss.

After an exhausting week of performing in New York, Charlotte would race back to Rose. They would saddle their horses and ride to Clover Hill, the new house Mr. Sully was building

*Miniature of Charlotte Cushman in
her twenties, by Rosalie Sully*

for his family. Charlotte was a passionate and confident rider and preferred a horse that responded to open ground by running flat-out as fast as it could go. Neither rider nor horse cared about conserving energy. Competition brought a flush to Charlotte's face, and she often challenged Rose to race. When Rose inevitably lost, Charlotte made it up to her with jewelry.

Rose expressed her love in a different key. For Charlotte's birthday in July, Rose gave Charlotte a miniature portrait of herself that Rose had worked on for weeks. Holding her own image cupped in her lap, Charlotte could see herself as Rose saw her: glossy chestnut hair, parted neatly in the middle and gathered at the nape of her neck, expressive, large dark eyes gazing straight out, unafraid, her mouth beginning to twist into a smile. It was not the most accurate portrait, Charlotte thought, but she looked beautiful.

———

Rose's love gave Charlotte confidence, and she decided to try what was acknowledged as the most difficult role in Shakespeare's canon: Hamlet. Sarah Siddons had first played Hamlet in 1776, but no American actress had done it successfully. It was a complicated, challenging role, essentially a character study, and she would have more than fifteen hundred lines. Hamlet is a philosopher, and she would need to show her understanding of the sense of Shakespeare's lines, lines that also held private meaning for her.

She debuted the role on May 13, 1844. The gas light gave off a smell like burning butter, and under the lights onstage an actress could feel like she was being roasted alive. In the half dark beyond the stage's hemisphere, prostitutes prowled through the men's upper gallery, their cries occasionally breaking the silence.

In the pit the audience passed applejack and peeled boiled eggs as they waited for the curtain to rise.

Who's there?
Nay, answer me: stand, and unfold yourself.

The audience continued talking through the first scene and most of the second. They talked as the ghost of King Hamlet glided across the stage in white greasepaint and rags, as Claudius entered holding Gertrude possessively by the arm. Finally, Charlotte strode onto the stage dressed as Hamlet. She wore tights and a loose doublet, her breasts disguised under heavy brocade, her large head bowed. Hamlet is a young man, and Charlotte's smooth woman's face made her a better fit for the role than a male actor of similar experience.

Charlotte was critical of actresses who took on breeches parts for the titillation the performances offered men. Their "limbs are apt to cling helplessly together," she wrote a fellow actor. Charlotte's Hamlet, however, was utterly masculine, but her actually being a woman made her love scenes especially effective; they were, wrote one critic, "of so erotic a character that no man would have dared indulge in them." Some critics who came to see her Hamlet said she was more convincing playing a man onstage than playing a woman in life.

Both audiences and critics appreciated the way she interpreted Hamlet. A reviewer in the entertainment rag *Amusements* would later write that Charlotte "appreciates the influence of the supernatural upon [Hamlet's] mind, she does not therefore, fall into the error of representing him as one who is merely playing a part . . . she enters into his melancholy." Privately, Charlotte was herself melancholy, despite her success. Her love for Rose had deepened. It wasn't enough to spend every day together; she wanted a household with Rose, even a family. Instead, in public she had to pretend that Rose was just a friend. Dressed as a young man, she stood as if naked before the audience, pleading, "O, that this too too solid flesh would melt, / Thaw and resolve itself into a dew!"

As a result of her success as Hamlet, by Christmas Charlotte had almost saved enough money to go to London. Rose was supportive, and as a Christmas present she gave Charlotte a diary. Inside the front cover of the pocket-sized book was the phrase "for persons of business." It was bound in bloodred cloth with marbled endpapers, and inside was a blank page for every day of the year, to record "interesting daily occurrences and future engagements."

Although Charlotte confided her plans to Rose, she concealed them from her family as long as she could. Because she was the family breadwinner, all her earnings were meant to be committed to paying room and board for Mary Eliza, Susan, and Ned. Her brother Charles's earnings as a salesclerk were only enough to support himself. Charlotte, as a "person of business," took her responsibility seriously, recording every expenditure, from cabs to penny candy for her little nephew.

Still, since talking with Macready, she had kept back some of her money for herself, putting it away secretly for a transatlantic passage. Rose would not be joining her. Charlotte promised the trip would be only six months, assuming that by then she would know if she'd succeeded or failed.

To some extent, her success would depend not only on her own talent but on the social circles who could put her in contact with the right people. She was a fiercely devoted friend and correspondent, and despite the fact that she often wrote half a dozen letters a day (recording every one in her diary), most of her letters began with some form of apology for not having written sooner. Some of these friends, like Macready, were connected directly with the theatre world, but she also now had a large, devoted circle of women friends who promoted and supported one another.

Charlotte's devotion as a friend did not mean she was uncritical, however, and marriages often got in the way of her friendships with other women. In Philadelphia, she had been overjoyed to meet the famous Fanny Kemble through a local circle of women artists there. Fanny had been her idol since childhood, a British actress who had overwhelmed audiences on both sides of the Atlantic with her tragic beauty. She allowed Charlotte into her inner circle, even confiding in Charlotte about her miserable life with her husband, Pierce Butler, a Southern gentleman she had married without knowing he owned a plantation worked by hundreds of slaves. Pierce's cruelty had driven her to seek a divorce, but without proof of his infidelity she was trapped.

Charlotte had learned a few things from her friends in the Bowery: The only way Fanny could get a divorce was to catch Pierce Butler in the act. And the only way to do this would be to hire a woman willing to seduce Fanny's husband and then bear witness against him in court. Thinking to help, Charlotte spoke about this idea to Fanny, who was horrified. Charlotte was thrust out of Fanny Kemble's circle of intimates as quickly as she had been brought in.

Charlotte thought marriage between men and women was foolish. Though she believed it was a covenant with God, she also believed that very few women should enter into it. For most of her friends, marriage was not a love match but an economic necessity, or at least a confusing combination of the two. One "bold and impulsive" friend married a man Charlotte thought "narrow" and "strange" and lost her joie de vivre. It pained her that friends often shut her out once they were coupled. Charlotte and Rose had also discussed committing to each other in a kind of marriage ceremony, but Charlotte found herself distracted by other women. She felt herself possessed by one singer's beautiful, expressive face, and in the diary Rose had given her, she noted other "exquisite" actresses she met in New York.

Charlotte was still traveling nearly every day between New York and Philadelphia, where she was finishing up her contract with the Walnut Street Theatre. In New York, she continued acting opposite Macready, who had promised to perform in a benefit to raise money for Charlotte's trip to London. She had bought a ticket on a ship aptly named the *Garrick*, after a famous actor, and had very little left over. She paid $100 for the ticket, a large outlay considering that her mother's board was $10 a month and that the exchange rate was more than five dollars to one pound. Most of her salary went to her family, and she had hired a maid. Sallie Mercer was an intelligent, literate, African-American girl of around fourteen. Sallie's mother was hesitant to let her daughter travel to London, but Charlotte reassured her that she and Sallie would be safe.

As she neared her departure date, Charlotte began to have misgivings about leaving Rose and her family behind. She became ill and jumpy. Thankfully, the weather in New York was so terrible it made her eager to go. One morning Charlotte woke at 6 a.m. thinking someone was calling her. The rain pounded in such a fury against her leaky window it sounded "as though the flood gates of heaven were opened." Charlotte huddled in her apartment all morning. She took the train all the way to Philadelphia that afternoon, only to discover that the show was canceled. Another theatre refused to pay her money she was owed. Frustrated, she scribbled in her diary that she couldn't wait to "get away from this horrid place."

She had exhausted herself working to make money for her trip. On a typical week, Charlotte played Portia on Wednesday, Lady Macbeth on Thursday, Goneril in *King Lear* on Friday,

Queen Elizabeth on Saturday. Still, she made time for a widening circle of friends, and sometimes was their benefactor. When one friend suddenly fell ill, Charlotte lent her husband money for medical expenses. (When the poor woman died a day later, her husband returned the three dollars.)

As the time for her departure to London neared, she and Rose began to make plans to commit to each other in a secret ceremony. Charlotte bought Rose a ring, and they agreed that, though they did not have a marriage contract, they would be married.

Charlotte spent the rest of the month tying up loose ends: collecting money owed to her, making sure her clothes and costumes were repaired and ready for London. Sallie sewed tassels and braided trim on Charlotte's silk-linked handbag, and Charlotte bought Sallie a new hat and gloves for the journey. Then on Friday, July 5, a little more than two weeks short of her twenty-eighth birthday, Charlotte took a cab to Rose's house, had dinner with her family, and spent the night. The next morning, she and Rose were privately married. "Slept with Rose," she giddily recorded in her diary. "Married." As a wedding gift, Rose gave her a tiny, coin-shaped portrait of Fanny Kemble, whom Charlotte still admired, attached to a tightly woven bracelet of Rose's light brown hair. A week later Charlotte and Rose slept together again. Afterward, Charlotte went home and spent the afternoon burning letters she didn't want her mother stumbling on while she was away.

Hoping to spend her ocean voyage improving her mind, Charlotte filled her suitcases with books. She chose authors who might be talked about in London's high society, including Mme.

de Staël, eighteenth-century France's most celebrated female intellectual (ironically, a famous letter writer); the economist Adam Smith; Charles Darwin, whose book *The Voyage of the Beagle* had become a bestseller (Charlotte listed his name in her diary under the heading "imagination unchecked"); and the Romantic poets Robert Southey, William Wordsworth, and Alfred, Lord Tennyson, whose poems made her curious about "nature-worship" and "pantheism." Like the Romantics she admired, Charlotte often saw her passions reflected back to her in nature: in cloudburst, tempest, and the sudden reemergence of the sun after a storm.

In early October 1844, Charlotte performed in a benefit performance for Macready, and he had promised to perform in hers the following day. In the morning, however, she discovered with horror that Macready had sailed to London in the night. She scrambled, managing to find an actor she had performed with before, George Vandenhoff, but he was not as big a name and she fumed over the money Macready had lost her.

On October 26, Charlotte boarded the *Garrick* to set sail for Liverpool. Sallie Mercer accompanied her, though she sailed in a separate, third-class berth. When Mary Eliza discovered Charlotte had been putting aside money in secret, she was furious, but she agreed it was a good idea. Mary Eliza had her own reasons for wanting Charlotte out of the country. Someone had been gossiping about Charlotte's relationships with women. They'd found out about her marriage to Rose and also about a flirtation with a young woman named Lizzie Gardette. "I have always said that time'll show whether I deserved all the unkind feeling that has been believed and harbored against me," Charlotte later wrote to her mother, "and I think time will show it."

The boat shoved away from the dock with a great bellow, and the passengers watched as New York became an island and then a horizon and then disappeared from view. As Manhattan faded, Charlotte wrote a quote from Longfellow's novel *Hyperion* onto the front of her diary: "Look not mournfully into the past, go forth to meet the dark and shadowy future without fear and with a manly heart."

In her berth, Charlotte opened her trunk to begin unpacking. In her luggage, alongside dresses, gloves, shawls, books, and a few precious pencils for writing in her diary lay a clutch of apples: Golden Russet, Golden Pippin, Carpenters. She planned to save the seeds to plant with Rose at Clover Hill when she returned.

Immediately, Charlotte felt nauseated. Like a woman gripped by morning sickness, she was wrung by competing urges to seal herself in her bed and climb up and out onto the deck to gulp fresh air. Every time she thought of home it made her "more wretched." Rose's sister Blanche had warned her that when she was seasick she "could not think of anything at all," yet Charlotte couldn't stop thinking. She heard Rose's voice as plainly as if she stood in front of her. "I see Rosalie in her painting room," she wrote miserably in her diary. "I hear her sigh for her absent friend and spirits fall. I feel almost her arms about me . . . I wonder what I should do without her, I would not care or wish to have another home, deprived of her or of her affection."

Charlotte had rarely had so much time to think, and she didn't like it. She worried that Rose would forget her or fall in love with someone else. She worried she would fail and this would all have been for nothing. She cried, feeling like her "heart would break."

Sallie was also miserably seasick, and they took turns taking care of each other. Once Charlotte had to rush to Sallie's room to help her close the porthole. Sallie had been vomiting, and one of her bunk mates had opened the porthole for fresh air, not realizing that when she did the water would rush in. Another night Charlotte felt so sick she begged Sallie not to leave her alone and fell asleep on Sallie's knee. She dreamt she was in the front room at home sitting on the sofa. Rose was by her side with her arm around her neck, cheek brushing her cheek, then Rose's lips brushing hers. "I truly believe if I had her in my arms at this moment I could press the breath out of her body," she wrote when she woke, yet in the dream something was wrong. Rose was mysteriously sad, and like Washington Irving's Rip Van Winkle Charlotte felt she had been away a long time.

In the morning, she ate breakfast on the deck sitting on a coil of rope, for once "not sea sick but sick of the sea." Two weeks into the voyage, Charlotte discovered that if she stayed on deck in the fresh air as much as possible, she could avoid the worst of her sickness. She got in the habit of walking the deck in any kind of weather.

One evening when the captain warned her of a coming storm, she decided to keep reading, rather than go down to her putrid berth. The squall came quickly. Before she had a chance to race belowdecks a giant wave reared up over the side of the ship and crashed down on her.

Blinded by the water, she thought she had been swept overboard. The wave shook her like a doll, knocking her off her feet and across the ship, where she lodged under the bulwark and stuck there. The bulwark, it turned out, was all that saved her from being thrown into the sea. Panicked sailors pried her out "half-drowned" and took her, shivering, below deck, where someone gave her dry clothes. Even then she was still "a little afraid," reminded of almost drowning off Long Wharf when she was a girl. But soon she regained her composure, even cracking jokes. "I was," she wrote in a letter to her mother, "the most dripping young woman you ever saw."

The next day, the mood of the sea had changed completely; the sky was clear and "glaringly beautiful." Charlotte, in a lilac dress with a shawl wrapped around her shoulders in the early morning chill, walked on the deck shading her eyes from the sunlight reflecting off the water. Looking up, she saw in the pale sky a few "fleecy" clouds and the slender new moon "in its first quarter." Over the side she saw what she took to be a good sign: porpoises jumping from the water "and bringing a beautiful wake behind them." Taking breakfast with the captain in the wheelhouse, round and windowed on all sides like a goldfish bowl, she could see the ocean surrounding her. She was the first passenger to hear the botswain shout out, "Land ho!"

The shout brought everyone on deck, and Charlotte saw with alarm that they were within a mile of Fastnet Rock and speeding toward it. Fastnet Rock marked the southernmost point of Ireland, but with no lighthouse to guide ships around it, many crashed there, within sight of land. Thankfully the *Garrick* sailed deftly around it, and soon they were journeying past Wales. Looking up at the white cliffs where "the foam there curls / And stretches a white arm out like a girl's," Charlotte thought how close she'd come to being a body washed up on that shore.

chapter nine

Enemies Abroad

———— • • ————

What fairer seal
Shall I require to my authentic mission
Than this fierce energy?—this instinct striving
Because its nature is to strive?

—Robert Browning, "Paracelsus"
(copied in Charlotte's diary)

The *Garrick* docked in Liverpool in November 1844, and before heading to London Charlotte spent a few days in Manchester with a couple she'd met on the ship. Although she'd made friends on board, Charlotte knew that most of the British people she would meet looked down on Americans as unmannered roughs. Charles Dickens had recently published his scathing *American*

Notes, and Charlotte had made the mistake of bringing his new novel *Martin Chuzzlewit* on board. In the novel a young rogue is punished by being forced to immigrate to America. She'd also heard many "disgusting" arguments between American and British passengers during the trip and found herself acting in the role of cultural ambassador—not just for her country but for her profession. One Englishwoman told her how surprised she was to discover Charlotte was an actress. "Whether she means it as a compliment or not," Charlotte wrote in exasperation, "I cannot know."

In Scotland, she went out riding every day. One afternoon, riding over the hills, she was stopped cold by the sight of a fox hunt. It was a scene of violence and beauty that could have been painted by Turner. Men in red coats and white breeches tucked inside tall black boots bent low over their horses' necks to follow the hounds racing across the landscape, its natural beauty punctured by long, slim smokestacks rising along the horizon.

When she returned to the house, there was a letter waiting for her. Macready wanted her to come to Paris, where his leading lady, the beautiful Helen Faucit, had just dropped out of a show. Charlotte relished the chance to turn her onetime friend down and knew it was a bad idea to debut as the replacement for an actress famed for her good looks. She immediately rejected his offer. He wrote back, "quite ill-tempered," saying she was "taking an irreversible step," and the next day sent a man from London to persuade her. But Charlotte remained firm, still resentful of him for standing her up at her benefit. When she read later in the newspaper that some small accident had kept him from traveling to Paris as he'd planned, she had a good laugh.

Finally arriving in London, Charlotte and Sallie moved into modest rooms in Covent Garden, and lived simply, proud they could make "a pound of mutton last three days." Charlotte went out every day to look for work, introducing herself to all the important theatre managers, who rejected her. She discovered that success in America not only carried little weight here but also might work against her, as the British were suspicious of American tastes.

When Charlotte heard that J. M. Maddox was looking for actors for the Princess Theatre, and that he had recently hired an American, Edwin Forrest, she put her letters of reference in her purse and went to see him.

At the theatre, Maddox invited her into his office, where he sat surrounded by portraits and mementos of the most famous British actors of the age, including Charlotte's former costars Junius Booth and William Macready. Charlotte showed Maddox her references and clippings of her best reviews, but he, too, said no. He even suggested she might be too ugly to be an actress. Charlotte gathered her papers and started to leave but turned again in the doorway, fixing Maddox with the furious stare of Meg Merrilies. Falling to her knees, she looked up, raising a fist: "I know I have enemies in this country," she thundered in a voice cracking with emotion, "so help me—I'll defeat them!"

Maddox recognized at once the energy of Lady Macbeth and Meg's "prophetic spirit." "Hello," said Maddox to himself, "so help me, she's got the stuff in her." She was hired.

Maddox was known to be a difficult manager, a strong negotiator, and "obstinate" in anything to do with business. Even his star actors had to wheedle for a pay raise, causing some, like the actor George Vandenhoff, to call Maddox—who was Jewish and spoke with a strong Yiddish accent—a "Shylock." Charlotte, however, respected Maddox's toughness and knew she was also a strong negotiator. When her brother Charles joined her in London in May 1845, he reported to Mary Eliza that Charlotte was "looking very well and is in very good spirits. Actually she is surrounded by friends who consider her the beau ideal of everything that is great . . . pleading a case of Mr Maddox: in the open [air], energizes her in an extraordinary manner." Maddox in turn respected her vitality and stubbornness, two qualities she shared with her new American costar, Edwin Forrest.

If Charlotte was at a disadvantage because of her looks, Forrest had risen to fame thanks to his. As a youth, Forrest had made his debut in a female role, when the actress playing a captive odalisque suddenly fell ill. But he grew up, and up, and up, reaching a height of five-foot-ten, taller than most men, and so thickly muscled he was described as "the Farnese Hercules," after the famous statue. "Sardonically handsome," he wore his long dark hair swept back; bushy sideburns nicknamed muttonchops framed his face, and he chose costumes that exposed his strong and shapely arms and legs.

As an actor, however, his reviews were mixed. The American critic William Winter described Forrest as an actor with "iron repose, perfect precision of method, immense physical force, capacity for leonine banter, fiery ferocity and occasional felicity of elocution." But critics sometimes complained of his "stentorian" tone, more lecturing than levitating, and unclear pronunciation that made Shakespeare difficult to understand. He had tremendous power, however, and was "utterly unselfish" with his energy onstage. His brawn at times overwhelmed his brains, making him look like some "vast animal bewildered by a grain of genius."

Still, Forrest was America's darling, the most famous actor they had yet produced. He had performed in Europe once before, and rumors of his success helped him make a fortune when he returned to America. Charlotte suspected, however, that Forrest's manager had paid audiences and critics to make Forrest seem more successful than he was.

Charlotte had negotiated with Maddox to let her play Romeo if she first played Lady Macbeth opposite Forrest. Maddox clearly expected the two Americans to have good chemistry, but he was wrong. The Forrest/Cushman *Macbeth* opened to mixed reviews. Forrest's Macbeth seemed strangely milquetoast, cowed by Charlotte's energetic Lady Macbeth. The more she pushed the less he resisted; even his tone was subdued. "It was something worse than ridiculous," a critic wrote, "to hear a man in such a great part as Macbeth—the sport of passion—the agent of supernatural powers—speak as cooly and easily as if his conversation were not upon treason and destiny, but upon the state of the weather." Another critic called Forrest's performance "the most unsatisfactory, the most inconclusive performance . . . known to the higher drama of this country." Londoners were unimpressed by Forrest's brawn and scandalized by his pronunciation. In a culture where caste and accent were synonymous, Forrest's American-ese made him sound—unforgivably—like a laborer pretending to be a king.

Though Charlotte was furious at Forrest for what she perceived as laziness, her own performance was surprisingly well received. Critics thought she feelingly evoked the "emptiness of ambition" and the "agony of gratified desire." One dissenting observer was so startled by her physical strength he wondered whether Charlotte might haul off and hit her husband, but generally London reviewers thought she was one of the best Lady Macbeths they had ever seen and crowned her the new Sarah Siddons. Charlotte thought that, considering the English "don't like Americans in the newspapers," she had done well.

The news of Charlotte's success quickly crossed the Atlantic to her home country, much to Walt Whitman's annoyance—he chastised Americans for failing to recognize her greatness sooner and was annoyed that the British seemed to be trying to claim her as their own. "Charlotte Cushman is *no* 'second Siddons,'" he retorted in a column for the *Brooklyn Eagle*, "she is *herself*, and that is far, far better!" Furthermore, she was "ahead of any player that ever yet trod the stage. Fanny Kemble, Ellen Tree, Miss Phillips, &c.—Macready, Kean, Kemble &c.—all had, or have, their merits; all played well, and their acting has afforded many an intellectual man and woman a rich treat. But Miss Cushman assuredly bears away the palm from them all, men and women."

Every evening Charlotte spent hours next to the flickering light of her lamp, reading and rereading old letters from Rose. She wrote to Rose almost daily but received nothing in return. She even wrote to Rose's father hoping to find out what was wrong, but still nothing. She noted gloomily in her diary every day that passed without a letter.

Charlotte was deeply homesick. Hoping to convince her family to join her abroad, she wrote a long letter to her mother, enclosing her press clippings as proof of her "brilliant and triumphant success in London." The ecstatic reaction of the press was "far beyond my most sanguine expectations and in my most ambitious moments I never dreamed of the success that awaited me." She was so popular, she wrote, she never went anywhere with "fewer than six people." She didn't mention late nights spent crying over Rose, tussles with Forrest and Macready, and the near failure with Maddox. "I have done more than any American has done in London. I truly have," she wrote. "No American has ever succeeded as I have. And though my heart bounds for it, yet I feel so sick for home I hardly know what to do." When she finally finished the letter, it was 3 a.m. "Play Lady Macbeth tomorrow," she signed off wearily. "I have hardly the strength to hold my head up."

Charlotte's performances continued to pack the theatre through the cold winter weather, and Maddox eagerly signed her on for the season, but the success was bitter on her tongue. She'd finally gotten a letter from Rose, which revealed that Thomas Sully had banned his daughter from having any further relationship with Charlotte. It seemed that a mutual friend had been gossiping about Rose and Charlotte's not-so-innocent relationship, and word had gotten back to Thomas Sully. If he had suspected that their relationship was romantic before, the fear of public exposure made him act now. Rose returned the portrait Charlotte had commissioned of herself for Rose to hang in her bedroom.

Instead of winning the admiration of her family and friends, instead of letters congratulating her on her hard-won success, Charlotte received criticism from her mother and chilly silence from Thomas Sully, a man she had called "father." And Rose did not put up a fight.

When Mary Eliza excoriated her for dragging the Cushman family name through the mud, Charlotte responded as a mother might to a petulant child. "I have not slept for three nights and look like a ghost," she fumed. She had been looking forward to congratulations, she wrote, not more malicious gossip. The argument with her mother continued for weeks, sapping Charlotte's energy and distracting her from her work. In early spring Charlotte received a final goodbye letter from Rose. Heartbroken, she went into mourning, not only for her lost love, but for the life they'd imagined together at Clover Hill. Still, the length of the ordeal lessened the blow—so did a new flirtation with a young woman who occasionally spent the night (telling her parents she was trapped by a snowstorm). For more company, Charlotte bought herself a dog and threw herself into her work. She was busy planning her next big role: Romeo. In preparation, she wrote to her sister, Susan, with clear instructions: she was to join her in London. Charlotte needed a Juliet.

chapter ten

Lady Romeo

———— ✦ ✦ ————

Casting Susan as Juliet had been Charlotte's
idea, and Maddox agreed, despite his skepti-
cism. Susan was pretty and feminine, with large
greenish-brown eyes and dark brown hair she
wore parted in the center like her sister. She was shorter and
slimmer than Charlotte, and her time at the Park had made her
into a fine "walking lady" (a kind of acting jack of all trades).
The idea of two sisters playing Romeo and Juliet was a novel
one. In another twist, Charlotte also demanded that they work
with the full text of the play, rather than the bowdlerized version from David Garrick that had been in fashion for decades.
In the Garrick version, Juliet wakes before Romeo dies and the
lovers are given "a mess of dialogue from [Garrick's] own pen,"

which, one critic wrote, "the best epithet for is balderdash." Charlotte, an American, insisted on a purity and fidelity to the original that Shakespeare no longer enjoyed in his own land.

At the time, it was a controversial choice. Other actors in the production "expressed in no uncertain terms the difficulty the 'original text' was giving them." They saw Charlotte as a pushy American, and considered the restoration of Shakespeare's text not in terms of purity, but as a regression to something "primitive." While Charlotte and Susan rehearsed, their fellow actors complained about them behind their backs, deriding them as "American Indians." But Charlotte continued to insist that they perform the play as written, even if that meant the whole company of actors would have to memorize new lines.

In the end, she got her way. The controversy over the production and the unusual pairing of two sisters in the lead roles made for a good story and on opening night the theatre was packed.

As a gesture of goodwill, William Macready sent Charlotte a dagger from one of his own performances with a note of encouragement. The superstition was that stage daggers never went dull, if kept in constant use. Before taking the stage on opening night, she slid the dagger into its sheath and belted it around her waist. In her dressing room she pulled on tall boots and smoothed her tunic of gold velvet. She had cut her hair short and curled it so that it fell in boyish waves around her ears. Susan was costumed in a tight-waisted, bare-shouldered dress of bridal white.

"Love is a smoke," Romeo declares at the start of the play, a troubled sea "nourish'd with lovers' tears." Though Garrick's version cut out Romeo's love affair with a girl named Rosaline, Charlotte had restored it for a reason. In Romeo's first lines,

Charlotte "disclosed that ardent, passionate disposition that waited but for the opportunity to break forth with irresistible violence, so that the first scenes contained the whole possibility of the tragedy." Critics approved of the choice.

The British audience also appreciated Charlotte's clear enunciation of Shakespeare's lines and her lack of a strong American accent. She had learned to speak well growing up among upper-class New Englanders and could pass for someone high-class. She had perfected the effect by copying Macready's accent. In fact, wrote one jokester, she even looked a bit like him: "the bend of the knee, slight sneer of the lip / the frown on the forehead, the hand on the hip / in the chin, in the voice, 'tis the same to a tittle, / Miss Cushman is Mr. Macready in little."

Charlotte was a convincing swordsman; she dueled like someone "to the manor born." During a fight scene with Tybalt, Charlotte hit her opponent's sword so hard that his weapon went flying downstage toward the audience. The pit erupted in cheers. "Miss Cushman is the one person we have seen who can handle a sword in stage combat so as not to make the encounter seem ridiculously prearranged," marveled one critic, "and at the same time give the affray the appearance of reality without savageness."

Her passion for Juliet also gave the appearance of reality, though with her sister as her costar, she was protected from further salacious gossip. Women found her Romeo an ideal lover: impulsive, sensitive, courageous, and cavalier. This sentiment was put best by an anonymous female fan: "Charlotte Cushman is a very dangerous young man."

Men, too, were moved by Charlotte's Romeo. Audiences

were used to seeing plays that emphasized men's capacity for savagery, but she showed them something new. When Charlotte discovered Juliet dead in a tomb, she did not merely hold the cold, dead hand, as others did, she crushed Juliet in her arms and wept freely. As Romeo, Charlotte revealed emotions men were not supposed to express in public. Her Romeo even made critics uncharacteristically self-reflective: "The character of Romeo is one which every man of sentiment takes to himself, and estimates according to his own feelings and impulses," wrote one observer. "Perhaps a more intellectual and at the same time a more theatrically effective performance has never been witnessed," enthused another.

Both men and women met her with flowers at the stage door.

Actors were sometimes criticized for making "points," or playing just for the big scenes, which made the story seem disconnected and artificial. But Charlotte, as the *Times of London* wrote, gave the play "the vivifying spark, whereby the fragments are knit together and become an organized entirety." It was this coherence, Coleridge claimed, that characterized the best interpretations of Shakespeare. She clearly saw Romeo as "an impetuous youth whose whole soul was absorbed into one strong emotion and whose lips must speak with the inspiration of his heart," not merely a "fine speech maker" or maudlin "stage-lover." In her hands he was "a creative, a living breathing ardent human being."

A few, however, were furious that Charlotte would try to "ape a man" onstage. Women had played Romeo before, but the goal was to titillate the men in the audience, who enjoyed seeing a pretty actress in a short tunic. Charlotte, however, acted like a man rather than a woman in tights, besting men at swordplay. Then, when her chivalric Romeo collapsed weeping in the final scene, she gave men in the audience the dangerous impression it was okay to do the same.

A controversy broke out in the press and between audiences and critics. Charlotte might "split the ears of the groundlings," wrote one of these critics, referring to the working-class audience who cheered Charlotte on from the pit, but he still believed she was nothing but a male "impersonator." Eventually even Queen Victoria weighed in. The young queen declared that while Charlotte "entered well into the character" of Romeo, no one would have ever imagined her a woman, her figure and voice being so masculine.

The one thing everyone agreed on was that Charlotte made a convincing man. The performance was complete. When a joker in the audience faked a sneeze during one of Charlotte's love scenes, she stopped the performance. Most actors would have ignored it, but Charlotte, still in character, led Juliet off-stage "as a cavalier might lead a lady from a place where an insult had been offered her," then returned to the stage and commanded: "Some man must put that person out, or I shall be obliged to do it myself." The offender was lifted up by the crowd and carried away. "The audience rose en masse and gave three cheers for Miss Cushman," who then went offstage to retrieve her Juliet and continued the play "as though nothing had happened."

Charlotte had swagger, or what the Italians called "sprazze-tura," a kind of studied nonchalance. As Romeo, she walked like a man, spoke like a man, moved her body with the confidence of someone used to taking up space. The most manly thing about her was her sense of freedom.

In fact, some argued, she was a better man than most men. Her love speeches had a poetic cadence that, they argued, no male actor could achieve. Alternately the chivalric cavalier and the tender lover, she was perfect in each. One reviewer declared her Romeo was one of the "most remarkable pieces of acting ever witnessed." Another wrote that, after seeing Charlotte Cushman, "lovemaking, as practiced by the other sex" would seem "a very stale, flat, and unprofitable affair."

As Charlotte's fame increased, she attracted more of London's rich and famous to the theatre. One night, Charlotte heard that an important critic was there to see her: James Sheridan Knowles, a former actor, had become one of the most famous living playwrights in the world. His opinion meant something. Knowles was steeped in Shakespeare, borrowing from *Othello*, *Titus Andronicus*, and *Winter's Tale* in his own work. From the stage Charlotte could see him, recognizable in his high-necked white shirt, black suit, black silk cravat, and shawl-collared coat. He had a dimpled chin, winged black eyebrows that made him look elfin despite his advanced age, and deep-set, appraising eyes.

Knowles watched "with astonishment" as Charlotte threw herself on the ground to take the measure of an unmade grave. "There is no trick to Miss Cushman's performance," he later observed. "No thought, no interest, no feeling seems to actuate her, except what might be looked for in Romeo himself, were Romeo reality."

Charlotte reminded him of the famous British tragedian Edmund Kean, whose *Othello* was the stuff of legend. There are some transcendent moments in watching a play that stay with you always, pressed, as Shakespeare said of love, like a seal into wax. And as with falling in love, the impression stays with you even as the details fade. For Knowles, Kean's third act of *Othello* was one of these moments. The third act is when Othello kills Desdemona for what he believes is her infidelity. A moment later he discovers she was innocent and he is therefore a murderer. Ever since seeing Kean's interpretation, Knowles had hungered for another such moment, and it was with pure delight that he took in Cushman's Romeo. She was at least as good as Kean, he later wrote to a friend. In fact, he was tempted to say better. It was a performance "of topmost passion!—Not simulated passion—no such thing—real, palpably real! The genuine heart-storm was on—on in the wildest fitfulness of fury!—and I listened, and gazed, and held my breath, while my blood ran hot and cold."

Knowles could only assume the rest of the audience was responding as he was, but he couldn't tear his eyes away long enough to check. He watched, enrapt, until "a thunder of applause" brought him back to himself. He felt that as soon as Charlotte walked onstage everything about her "attest[ed] the lover." Knowles watched as Romeo tried and failed and tried again, with "aid of palm, and eye, and tongue," to tell Juliet how he felt.

Theatre was Knowles's life, and he felt Charlotte had

given him a great gift. "My heart and mind are so full of this extraordinary—most extraordinary performance," he wrote, "equal to the proudest of those which I used to witness years ago and for the repetition of which I have looked in vain until now."

By the spring of 1847 Charlotte was surprised to find herself welcomed into the London home of Samuel and Anastasia Laurence for their Sunday evening salons. The young couple surrounded themselves with artists and radicals, and Charlotte was the newest addition to their bohemian group. Samuel was a portrait painter, and his famous clients stared down at her as she entered his crowded sitting room.

The group modeled their salon after the radical thinker Charles Fourier, the man who had coined the term "feminism" around the time Charlotte was making her stage debut. Charlotte and Fourier shared the conviction that women should be allowed to hold a job, as well as a suspicion that marriage was primarily a legal agreement that did women no favors. Salons like the Laurences', in England and France, inspired the playwright Henri Murger's celebrated drama *Scènes de la Vie de Boheme*, and were a safe haven for people who wanted to move away from the mainstream.

Each week, the guests had plenty to talk about. In America, Whitman had used his pulpit at the *Brooklyn Eagle* to denounce America's invasion of Mexico and had been fined. Abolitionists worried about what a new Southern state would mean for their cause. One night, ensconced in an armchair, Charlotte listened to Jane Welsh Carlyle's arguments for women's right to hold property; she became friends with journalist and editor Mary Howitt, who was writing a long advocacy paper against capital punishment of women, and who soon took Charlotte under her wing. Howitt frequently wrote about her new actress friend in *Howitt's*, the journal she edited with her husband. Mary's feature on Charlotte and Susan—"the Misses Cushman"—helped make Charlotte even more of a celebrity. In it, she revealed Susan's teenage pregnancy and her husband's abandonment. Charlotte's "heart bled" for her sister, wrote Howitt, and she determined to help her make a new life: "Charlotte's was a character on which her sister, disappointed and heartbroken, could lean and from which she could derive strength."

This new explosion in the use and power of the popular press meant Charlotte's new writer friends were in high demand, and many women found jobs at newspapers and magazines, especially in New York and London. Mary Howitt immediately introduced her to other women writers, many of whom found her fascinating. She was a witty conversationalist, and continued to read voraciously even with her busy schedule. Though she was not particularly interested in politics, she continued to love literature—Jane Austen, George Sand—and poetry. She was young, intelligent, wildly talented, and self-supporting. "I am my own business-man," Charlotte liked to say. Soon, others came to see her as a kind of mascot for women's rights, and Charlotte was flattered by the attention.

But many of the women Charlotte found herself surrounded by were not only interested in her mind. They found her magnetic, and her strength intensely appealing. This made her both loved and hated. Jane Carlyle, a poet whose miserable marriage to the eminent critic Thomas Carlyle led her to rely heavily on her female companions, wrote bitterly that her intimate friend Geraldine Jewsbury was "all in a blaze of enthusiasm about Miss Cushman the Actress." Geraldine's letters were so full of praise of Charlotte that Jane wrote her a furious letter that she expected "will probably terminate our correspondence." Geraldine, in turn, was frustrated by these rivalries. She hoped that recent advancements in women's rights meant that women could live a normal life, and that if women were "taught not to feel their destiny manque if they remain single," they would not make themselves unhappy in bad relationships and could be better friends to each other.

Charlotte's new friendships were further complicated by the arrival of Eliza Cook, a gallant young writer whose poem "The Old Arm-Chair" had been published when she was just seventeen, and whose work was widely read and pirated on both sides of the Atlantic. One evening at the Laurences' Charlotte was deep in conversation when she saw a woman in her twenties striding through the crowd in a man's shirt, a skirt, and woolen cloak. The woman "rather sauntered than walked" over to the fire, where she pulled up a chair and put her feet up on the fender. Leaning back precariously, she shouted for a beer. Her dark ringlets cascaded messily over her collar, and Charlotte, catching her gaze, found herself staring into the girl's large blue eyes. Introducing themselves, Charlotte struck up a conversation, and Cook revealed that she had already seen Charlotte as Romeo and been so starstruck she wrote a poem about her.

Not since Rosalie Sully had Charlotte felt this strongly about a woman. They began going everywhere together, and Eliza was so energized by Charlotte's company she wrote more and faster than ever before, completing a manuscript in months. When Eliza's publisher delayed publishing the book, Charlotte wrote to admonish him. The volume, with a dedication to Charlotte, arrived in bookstores a few months later. One afternoon Charlotte and Eliza were out walking when they were caught in a sudden rainstorm. They sheltered under a tree, smelling the wet warmth of each other's bodies. Then Charlotte began to sing, her voice rising up through the branches, soft and sad. The song was one of Eliza's favorites, a Scottish ballad called "Jock O'Hazeldean," which her mother had sung to her when Eliza was a girl. Charlotte's voice was warm, worn, rough as the road the dead traveled on, shot through with wild longing.

The ballad tells the story of a woman pining for a lover she cannot have. Their love, forbidden, drives him away and he is now dead, forever beyond her grasp. Her parents try to force her to marry another young man in the village, but the day of the wedding the bride escapes through the veil, "ower the border and awa' wi' Jock O'Hazeldean." It was a song of love, outlawed.

Charlotte sent a copy of Eliza's poems to Geraldine Jewsbury, who read them feeling like she was meeting her own ghost. She wasn't impressed by the poems, judging the writer too in thrall to her subject to write well. "If you ever quarrel," she wrote to Charlotte cattily, Eliza "will write a much finer poem on you." Charlotte pretended to be ignorant of Geraldine's jealousy while consciously inflaming it. "I am not an angel but a wild cat," Geraldine warned her, "and I'll scratch you if I can't beat you."

Geraldine tried to temper her affection, knowing she would be "made miserable for it someday."

Charlotte and Eliza stayed together for nearly two intense years. And when Eliza finally felt Charlotte drifting away, it made her so anxious she became seriously ill. She searched Charlotte's face, finding signs that the woman she loved did not love her back. Charlotte had moved on, and it broke Eliza's heart.

By 1848 Charlotte had become famous and was playing Romeo to many women. "Darling," she wrote to a young actress named Sarah Anderton, whom she met during an engagement in Sheffield, "I love you. And that will give you courage, will it not? Looks of love have a more healing power with me than all the doctory stuff in the world," she wrote to Anderton in the winter of that year.

Charlotte also craved her own household and was happiest when surrounded by friends and family. Her brother Charlie, who had joined her in London shortly after she arrived, remarked that she never went anywhere except with an entourage. Charlotte had also convinced her mother to follow Susan to London, and now she had her whole family with her, even little Ned.

She and Susan continued to perform *Romeo and Juliet* to enormous crowds across Great Britain. With the help of Mary Howitt, Eliza (who remained her friend), Geraldine, and others, Charlotte became a household name.

Charlotte began to lease her image to make more money, and a Staffordshire figurine depicting Charlotte as a heroic Romeo with Susan leaning against her in a half swoon soon decorated mantelpieces across England. Newspapers rushed to publish etchings of her likeness. She encouraged the publicity but

half-joked to a friend about "the libels which have been perpe-
trated upon me in the way of engravings . . . I am made virtually
a hag." By the end of 1848 Charlotte seemed to know someone in
every circle. Her connections and visibility as an actress gave her
new power. When Charles Dickens received a letter from her, he
wrote to his friend Macready, "I ought to answer immediately."

Finally, the exhausting life on the stage lost its allure for
Susan. While touring in Liverpool, she caught the eye of a scien-
tist named James Sheridan Muspratt, and he soon proposed. She
would have to leave the stage to marry him, but despite the lost
income Mary Eliza urged her daughter to do it. Charlotte again
protested that Susan was not in love, and to marry anyway would
be to "sell her soul."

Young Ned did not like Muspratt, and Susan's new fiancé
was not eager to raise another man's son. Charlotte and Ned had
always been close—he called her Big Mama—and she was happy
to keep him with her. Charlotte played peacemaker between Ned
and Susan, reminding him that his mother had given birth to
him very young, when she was still a child herself. Finally, Charlotte wrote to the American government to have Ned's absent
father declared dead, and when the paperwork came through she
adopted him and he took the name of Cushman. Susan became
pregnant again shortly after her marriage, and Charlotte knew
Susan would never again go on the stage. It was time to find a
new Juliet.

chapter eleven

The Greatest American Actress

I have had a very interesting American visitor, Miss Cushman, the tragic actress—a very superior woman. They say she is an actress of great genius," wrote the celebrated playwright Mary Mitford when she first met Charlotte in 1845. Since her arrival in England, news of Charlotte's great talent had continued to spread throughout the British literati. Mitford's friend Elizabeth Browning was eager to meet her, as was Samuel Taylor Coleridge; his wife, Sara; and the American radical Lucretia Mott.

Once they did, people usually found that Charlotte lived up to the myth. Tall and commanding, she was a magnetic personality and a stunning conversationalist. During one meeting, she deeply impressed the radical abolitionist Thomas Wentworth

Higginson, who wrote to a friend, "What a wonderful creature Miss Cushman is . . . After producing her America may win pardon for a million half-alive women."

As her popularity began to grow, newspapers began to report on more than just her performances. One headline simply read "How Charlotte Cushman Made Her Fortune, $600,000." Soon, she was even famous enough to blackmail. The mother of one young woman claimed that Charlotte had sent her daughter a flirtatious note. She threatened to go public, but Charlotte met attacks on her reputation and livelihood with cold steel. "Of course the mother [meant] to intimidate me and mine," she wrote to her theatre manager about her would-be blackmailer. "They have made a mistake." She immediately spoke to a lawyer, declared the love note was forged, and produced several similar ones, all sent to people in the theatre by someone claiming to be her. If her enemies thought she was a "pantheress" only onstage, they were wrong.

Instead of settling down into her new role as one of London's social elite, Charlotte still burned with ambition. In the winter of 1848 she was celebrating the four-year anniversary of leaving America, and still yearned to prove herself to the country that had once ignored her. No other American was as celebrated or well known in England than she was; she had succeeded where Forrest and many others had failed, becoming the first American celebrity.

She planned her return to America with military precision. Charlotte wrote to Mr. Price, the new manager of the Park Theatre in New York, appealing to him as a fellow American and criticizing the "stupid farces" then dominating the London stage "which by constant repetition get loaded with the actor's own jokes. And so pass current." She casually name-dropped to prove that she was familiar with the American theatre scene, proclaiming how much she was looking forward to Helen Faucit's upcoming role (a serious part in a new comedy), and displayed her industry knowledge when she mentioned that she knew Edwin Forrest was making $3,000 a play, but that "most likely he will go to the Broadway Theatre. The Park was always too good for him."

"You seem to have no stars," she wrote, pointing out that Macready had not returned to America that season, and lamenting that with his long engagement elsewhere there will be "no stars to come to America in a long time." Charlotte positioned herself as the hero defending American theatre: "America hereafter will be the only ground for the drama," she boldly wrote. "Here it is dying out as fast as it possibly can." Europeans, she explained, were obsessed with French drama and short farces, and it was time for Americans to develop a "drama of our own." In England, "the axe has been laid at the root [of the theatre] and while two of their sickly branches are suffering one in a sort of isolated grandeur, the stem is dying fast! I see this more and more the longer I am here."

It was a stunning letter for a performer to write, much less a female one.

Charlotte understood her value as an American star—and she made sure others knew it. "I purpose coming to America in August next," she wrote to Price around 1848, "and shall begin to work in October." The plan, she stated, was simple: "Gallop through the country as fast as I can. And make as much money as I can." She demanded nothing less than what her male costars Forrest and Macready were making, "a clear half the house each night."

Charlotte's plans were coming together. There was just one complication: a new flame named Matilda Hays, "Max" to her friends. Max was a writer who had made a successful career as the English translator for George Sand. Sand was the nom de plume of the French writer Amantine Lucile Aurore Dupin, a prolific and popular novelist and playwright infamous for leaving her husband for an actress. Her subsequent affairs with both men and women were well publicized, and her translator was equally progressive in her relationships. Slim and tall, Max dressed like a man of letters in button-up shirts and bow ties.

At first, Charlotte wooed Max by convincing her to appear alongside her as her new Juliet. For a few months Charlotte gave Max acting lessons and they performed their budding love in public. Max initially agreed to the arrangement because she needed the money, but her interest in acting was temporary, and she quickly gave up the role for that of Charlotte's offstage wife. Their romantic relationship was never acknowledged by the press, who referred to them always as friends or acquaintances, when they mentioned Max at all. But it was not a secret. When Charlotte and Max went out together to parties or dinners it was as a couple, dressed nearly identically in collared shirts, ties, waistcoats, and skirts to the floor.

When the poet Elizabeth Barrett Browning met Charlotte and Max in Rome, she was disturbed and excited by their relationship.

"I forgot to tell you that we met Miss Cushman, the American actress," Elizabeth reported to her sister, Arabella. "She was with her Miss Hays." The two went everywhere together, she noted. "They live together, dress alike . . . it is a female marriage." Though Elizabeth was shocked by this, a sophisticated friend assured her the relationship was "by no means uncommon."

Female marriages, however, were expected to be chaste, and female passion was never discussed in public. A woman who loved other women too fiercely could be treated as a novelty, or, as the horrific novel *The Female Husband* warned, she could be hunted down and whipped in the public square. Charlotte and Max had to be careful. This would be particularly true in America, which was even more puritanical than Victorian England.

Max resisted going with Charlotte on the American tour because it would mean putting off the translation work she had already delayed. Ultimately, though, she gave in and Charlotte released to the press the news of her triumphant return to her native land. Newspapers in America reported giddily that Miss Cushman, "the greatest American Actress," was finally returning, accompanied by "her friend, Miss Hays."

The America Charlotte returned to in 1849 was more volatile than the one she had left. Former president Andrew Jackson's Indian Removal Act in 1830 had led to the state-sanctioned murder of nearly four thousand Cherokees and the displacement of many thousands more. Nearly eighty thousand white men were now traveling through what was once Indian land to reach gold country in the unincorporated lands of the Far West. The Mexican-American War had just ended, and many enslaved African-Americans were fleeing north on the Underground Railroad. The Seneca Falls Convention in upstate New York had rallied many thousands around women's rights. There, the writer and intellectual—and former slave—Frederick Douglass made an eloquent speech linking women's suffrage to universal suffrage for people of all races. And yet hostilities between the North and South were rising.

In New York, the Astor Place Riots shocked the country. The tragedy began in May with a feud between William Macready and Edwin Forrest over competing performances of *Macbeth*. Macready disliked Forrest. He thought the bombastic actor unrefined and brutish, but he failed to appreciate how much Forrest meant to his working-class supporters in America. When Macready disparaged Forrest in a newspaper, it sounded to American ears very much like the kind of insults they'd endured from the British since the nation's founding. The wealthy, British Macready represented everything the working-class audiences detested. Forrest was playing to a mixed audience at the Bowery, while Macready was performing at the new Astor Place Opera House, an opulent, expensive venue created expressly to keep out the lower classes. When some of Macready's supporters came to Forrest's *Macbeth* and hissed at him from the audience, it was the last straw. A group of Bowery Boys—always Forrest supporters—plotted to disrupt Macready's performance of *Macbeth* at the Astor Place Opera House. This protest, however, was met by the National Guard, whose presence inflamed the protest into a riot. Guardsmen fired on their own people, killing thirty.

If it was, as some said, a restaging of the Revolutionary War, it was also a struggle over whether the rich or poor would have the right to define American culture. Some called it "the Shakespeare Riot."

Perhaps because of the growing ideological divisions in America, the nation was hungrier than ever for theatre. As railroad lines extended into St. Louis, Chicago, Minneapolis, and farther west, theatre troupes found a new way to access the American interior. There was more money to be made by performing the same show in city after city than by casting, rehearsing, and mounting a new production every few weeks, and Charlotte planned to use this approach with her own work. She already had a repertoire of successful characters with Lady Macbeth, Meg Merrilies, Nancy, Hamlet, and Romeo, and once she cast the other parts she knew she could make the same great dish a hundred times without fail. She was recognized everywhere she went, and with railways and newspapers expanding far across the nation, her name and reputation traveled ahead of her. It was time for her talents to come home.

One rough, cold winter afternoon, a train nicknamed the *Hercules* was traveling from Logansport to Chicago on the Chicago and Great Eastern Railroad. It was, the captain recalled, a bad day for crossing the prairies "with the wind blowing over them as I believe it never blows anywhere else except off Lake Michigan." Suddenly, he received an order to hold the train at the station while two more cars were added to its load. The *Hercules* was strong enough, but the captain was baffled. He'd never received such an order before. Far in the distance a little engine towed the two additional cars toward the train. When they arrived, the *Hercules* passengers were surprised to see the great tragedienne Charlotte Cushman disembark with her attendants. She had missed a connection somewhere and needed to arrive in Chicago in time for that night's performance. She traveled in style, with her "belongings"—both her family and friends as well as her luggage and costumes—filling both cars.

Though the captain did his best with the late start, the headwinds got the better of him and "out on the open prairie, about four o'clock on the gray November afternoon, we came to a dead halt." The captain picked up his oil can and heaved the door open against the wind, struggling to reach the engine room, as a gust thrust him backward each time he made progress. Finally he gave up and dropped to his hands and knees, crawling back the way he'd come. "Presently," the captain recounted, "one of the brakemen, with his hat tied to his head with a stout scarf" to keep it from blowing away "came forward to tell me that Miss Cushman wished to see the engineer in the passenger car."

He declined, sending word that he was doing all he could and they'd be moving again soon. But then the fireman, Mike, whistled in his ear: "An it is herself that is coming now be jabers!" The captain looked out of the window, and there was Charlotte, advancing through the gale along the side of the train. "At first she walked majestically forward, the wind storm seeming to have no impact on her stout, erect figure; but soon she began to cling to the sides of the cars, her ample skirts blowing back, making anything but a graceful or dignified appearance." When she finally reached the cab, the captain and fireman helped her up inside it. Safe from the wind, Charlotte stormed about the delay. "She tried high tragedy with me," said the captain, but he assured her that the engine only needed time to rest: "After Hercules has had time to breathe a little I think he will take us on again. I imagine he will find working ahead of old Boreas," the Greek God of the North Wind and winter, "to be a harder matter than any of the labors of his immortal namesake." Charlotte was amused by the classical reference and could not hide her surprise that the captain was familiar with the old myths.

Warming to the task, Charlotte tried more "honeyed" words with the captain, who "felt the power of her personal magnetism." "She had put new life into me, and it seemed as if the Hercules drew strength from my touch, for the steam-gauge ran up to almost blowing-off." Charlotte went back to her car, grabbing the step guards just before she was blown past the train entirely.

As the train began to move, the captain looked back and saw Charlotte watching him through the top window of the smoking car. She nodded and smiled at him, "her great eyes agleam with excitement and a look of suppressed power in her face I never saw lined on any human countenance."

When they arrived in Chicago, Charlotte came to say goodbye. She asked the captain where he was staying and his room number and shook his "grimy" hand "as cordially as if it had been dressed in immaculate kid" leather. Half an hour later the captain was settling in to his rooms when a messenger arrived with two tickets to Charlotte's performance that night. The captain remembered until the end of his life watching Charlotte perform and seeing her notice him and nod from the stage.

Traveling from New York to Chicago to St. Louis, Charlotte continued to see success in each city, her popularity growing beyond even her imagination. She tried out a new role, Cardinal Wolsey in *Henry VIII*, and this, too, was a hit. When she turned east again for her triumphant hometown return to Boston, she was celebrated as an American hero. In Boston, she was delighted to be introduced to the poet Henry Wadsworth Longfellow. Just a few years earlier Charlotte had written lines from Longfellow's novel *Hyperion* in her diary, and now he was calling on her, writing a play for her to star in. The two became friends, bonding over their admiration of the German composer Mendelssohn, and their mutual friend Samuel Laurence. Longfellow and Max became acquainted as well, discussing literature in English and French. Longfellow's passion for his wife, Frances, bloomed as wildly as the lilacs outside their house, and he noticed, in contrast, that Max had a "vague sense of sadness . . . some bitterness, as of disappointment."

Charlotte, too, worried about Max's happiness, even as she could not ensure it. The decision to leave England had been painful. Some of Max's friends, suspicious of this new relationship, accused Charlotte of "selfishly sacrificing" Max's happiness to her own. One friend in particular behaved so inappropriately that Charles Dickens jumped in to defend Charlotte "very prettily," reminding the woman that Max's decision was none of her business.

Toward the end of the tour, Charlotte and Max posed for a photo as a souvenir. Dressed alike in bow ties and men's waistcoats, they look in opposite directions, tired and tight-lipped.

While privately struggling to keep her relationship together, publicly Charlotte was enjoying unprecedented levels of national fame. As Macready had predicted, the "foreign stamp of approbation" gave Americans the permission they needed to like her. She had become an "empress," "nodding but to be obeyed, smiling but to be worshipped." She was talented, intelligent, independent, and now rich, demanding equal pay to Macready and Forrest, two of the most famous actors in the world.

For the first time, America had a true celebrity of its own. Newspapermen dined out on her, reporting where she went and with whom. In Brooklyn, Walt Whitman reprinted a notice from the *Cleveland Plain Dealer* that Charlotte had been spotted leaving her hotel in the resort town of Sault Saint Marie in men's clothes. Whitman was delighted:

Miss Charlotte Cushman, who is spending a quiet vacation in that inspiring clime, astonished the guests of the St. Marie Hotel one morning by appearing equipped cap-a-pie in masculine attire—hat, coat, unmentionables and all. You who have seen her personation of 'Hamlet' can easily understand the grace and ease with which she wore her new 'toggery.' Here was a single motive of triumph; not a mere desire to astonish the dinner table, and then, like the ghost of Banquo, to vanish away and go back to petticoats and whalebone. No, she rode in it; and for ought that we can learn, had determined to wear it for the remainder of her days—at least, of her maidenhood.

Charlotte's cross-dressing was not a stunt, Whitman realized, it was an expression of her true self. Whitman also made a sly nod to Charlotte's sexuality, predicting she would continue dressing like a man for the rest of her life, or her maidenhood (which for a woman who loved other women was essentially the same thing).

Though Charlotte sought success, celebrity wore her down, and she sometimes felt like a "thousand mouths (were) feeding on me." She responded by surrounding herself with an entourage of female friends: ambitious, unorthodox artists like herself who longed for more freedom than they could find in America or in England. Soon, she had a new dream.

In Boston, she and Max befriended two new women: Grace Greenwood, the *New York Times*'s first female reporter, and an up-and-coming young sculptor named Harriet Hosmer. Hosmer had quickly fallen for Charlotte after seeing her as Romeo, and continued to see her perform as Lady Macbeth, Meg Merrilies, Hamlet, Queen Katharine in *Henry VIII*, and many others. The quartet called themselves the "Jolly Bachelors," and, not content merely to dream of artistic freedom, they decided to take the radical step of making a home together in Rome.

Charlotte had flirted with Bohemianism in England, but this would be her first attempt at creating her own artistic community. Artists and writers were flocking to Italy to live luxuriously in inexpensive villas and enjoy more personal and creative freedom than at home. Max imagined herself finishing the translation of George Sand's *La Petite Fadette*, which she had only been able to peck away at on tour. Grace had an idea for a novel, and Harriet would immerse herself in studying masterpieces of classical sculpture. It was less clear what Charlotte would do, but she believed she was done with the stage forever. At thirty-three she was independently wealthy and an international celebrity. What she wanted now was a home in Rome with Max and her closest friends around her.

chapter twelve

Rome

The buskers' cries followed Charlotte as she passed under the obelisk in the Piazza del Popolo, the People's Square. Turning onto the Via del Corso, Rome's busiest thoroughfare, she passed into the shade of candy-colored buildings that rose on either side. By the time Charlotte and her friends moved there in 1852, Rome had become a popular tourist destination. It was spring, and white, star-shaped blossoms emerged among the glossy leaves of mock orange trees. Music drifted out of open windows as Charlotte walked south, following the sound of water. Ten minutes later she arrived at Bernini's Fontana della Barcaccia at the foot of the Spanish Steps.

The steps were white and steep as the cliffs at Dover; pausing for breath at the top, one had a view from the muddy Tiber River to the crumbling travertine of the Colosseum. Clouds of swallows wheeled and shrieked like tragedians. Charlotte looked around her, at the streets of her new home. She now lived down the street from the Villa Medici, the former home of the powerful family who bankrolled the Renaissance.

Though she had retired from the stage for the time being, Charlotte continued working behind the scenes, using her fame to find patrons for her friends. She had moved to Rome with Max, Grace, and Harriet, but the community grew as she began to support more women artists, offering them a place to stay in Rome, extending loans, giving gifts, and writing letters on their behalf to her powerful connections. Under her care, the "Jolly Bachelors" flourished.

Growing up in Massachusetts, Harriet Hosmer endured tragedy early in her life. When she was a child, her mother and siblings all died suddenly, leaving her alone with her terrified father. A physician, he was desperate to protect his one remaining child from illness and created a strenuous daily exercise regimen for young Hattie. Dr. Hosmer raised her largely as he would a boy, and she grew up confident and strong. After she beat all the neighborhood boys racing up and down a nearby hill, they renamed it "Mount Hosmer" in her honor. She also showed early promise as an artist, starting with sketching and painting, then moving on to sculpture—which became her passion. Hattie knew that to become a great sculptor she needed to study live anatomy, which meant nude models. But as a woman she was not allowed to enter any of the academies let alone look at naked men and women. Finding the artistic climate of New England stifling, she begged her father to let her move with her new friend Charlotte Cushman to Rome. There, she argued, she could study classical sculpture, join the male artists in sketching from nude models, and be taken more seriously as a sculptor. Dr. Hosmer could not refuse.

Hattie's sculptures argued eloquently, if silently, for women's emancipation. Cleverly, she channeled her politics through a mythological lens—tackling classical subjects, as a man would, but with a twist. Her bare-breasted Medusa was captured halfway through her transformation, so that a gorgon's head sat atop a mortal woman's body. Her masterwork, however, was a statue of Beatrice Cenci, a character well known to nineteenth-century readers through Percy Bysshe Shelley's play *The Cenci*. In the tragic tale, Beatrice's father, Count Cenci, has his own sons murdered and keeps Beatrice captive, gets her drunk, and tries to convince her to participate in orgies with her own mother. When he tries to rape Beatrice, she kills him, and the very citizens who wished for the count's death hang her for her crime.

The most famous image of Beatrice to date was a portrait attributed to Guido Reni painted in 1600. It dwells on her weakness, depicting her as a barely adolescent girl wrapped in a bedsheet. Hattie's Beatrice, on the other hand, is older, more womanly. She lays on a pillow, her bedsheets wrapped around her like a goddess gown. One bare arm trails off the side of her bed, and she cradles a rosary in her hand, her fingers wrapped idly through its strands. Her face is partly obscured as she looks not at the viewer for help (as the woman in the Reni portrait does) but toward contemplation of the rosary. She seems at peace; the muscles, clearly visible in her arms, back, and neck, are relaxed. It is an image not of penitence but of release.

The other friend who joined Charlotte, Max, and Hattie in Rome was Sarah Jane Clarke. She wrote under the name Grace Greenwood and had become a successful novelist and the first female journalist at the *New York Times*. Her friend Nathaniel Hawthorne admired her novels, finding them sad, but beautiful. He hoped that after some time abroad she might decide to write something "with more sunbeams" in it. Her letters to him, he wrote, were "better than any man's." Hawthorne was suffering from writers' block so severe it gave him a "detestation of pen and ink." When she finally arrived in Rome, Grace found it so wonderful she wrote that he might find his inspiration there. She was right. When he and his wife, Sophia, finally came in 1858, the journey resulted in a novel, *The Marble Faun*.

The novel follows a group of women artists living together in Rome. In one scene the artist Hilda and her friend even discuss Beatrice Cenci. "Beatrice's sin may not have been so great," argues the friend; perhaps murdering her rapist should be considered "virtue" given the circumstances.

Hawthorne was deeply affected by Charlotte when he met her, and she was equally impressed with him. Although Hawthorne had previously sworn he would never sit for another portrait, when she asked him to do it (so she could have an image of him to hang in her house), he responded effusively, "After the impression of her own face which Miss Cushman has indelibly stamped on my remembrance, she has a right to do just what she pleases with mine."

The Jolly Bachelors seemed to charm nearly everyone who met them. When Hattie's father, Dr. Hosmer, came to check on her, the women in the house liked him so much they adopted him as one of their own and began calling him "Elizabeth." He didn't mind a bit.

A few people, however, found a group of women living together distasteful, and their artistic ambitions suspect. For example, the sculptor and poet William Wetmore Story had made his home in Rome years earlier and considered it his territory. He wrote back to friends in America about the disgusting spectacle he thought Charlotte and Hattie made, dressing in men's pants and ties and riding far and fast across the fields like young men. He hid his dislike under seeming concern about the damage they were doing to their reputation—and to that of all Americans living in Italy. Hattie, he wrote, "takes a high hand here in Rome, and would have the Romans know a Yankee girl can do anything she pleases, walk alone, ride her horse alone, and laugh at their rules." Apparently, on at least one occasion the spectacle of Hattie riding alone created such a riot that the police had to intervene. But Story was biased against women artists in general; he believed Hattie was a good copyist, "but if she has inventive powers as an artist . . . will not she be the first woman?"

The group of expatriates living full-time in Rome was small, and Charlotte often met Story at parties. He scoffed at her habit of entertaining the guests with ballads, complaining that her voice sounded savage and too masculine. He called Charlotte's

Harriet Hosmer with workmen circa 1850s

group of artists a "harem-scarem," and when his friend Henry James visited Rome, James also mocked them, as the "white marmorean flock." Part of this dislike was the fact that the women in Charlotte's circle were not only gifted artists but also successful ones. Story and his friends were not used to competing with women, and they didn't like it.

Others, however, including Elizabeth and Robert Browning, found the Jolly Bachelors exciting, and Charlotte's home soon became the epicenter of social life for expat artists living in Rome. In an echo of Christina Rosetti's poem *Goblin Market*, one guest felt that anyone who sat down at their "Apician feasts" bore their sweetness on his lips forever. Charlotte, Max, Grace, Hattie, and their new friend Virginia Vaughan became known as the "Five Wise Virgins," and only the brightest and most fascinating were invited to their regular Wednesday night dinners. The conversation was brilliant, the politics radical. Guests left inspired, having had "contact with every form and kind of art—quickened by the peculiar eagerness of all who were in a far and strange land."

One evening, a starstruck young man begged Charlotte to sing. She laughed it off at first, claiming she had lost her voice years ago, but sat down at the piano and began to play quietly, "just touching the keys so as to give a background to the picture." Then she sang, "paint[ing] on the air the old ballad of Chevy Chase with such marvellous dramatic power that the whole story became real." Charlotte sang ballad after ballad, finishing with an old Russian hymn, tears falling down her face until finally she broke off, bowing her head to weep.

Charlotte and her friends wanted to expand the possibilities for all women. They befriended women's rights reformers, like Jane Carlyle and Lucretia Mott, who believed that friendships, not marriage, formed the core of a woman's emotional life. Charlotte went further, on one hand believing that marriage was sacred and on the other hand convinced that marriage was, for most women, more of an evil than a good, even a form of slavery. The artist colony Charlotte and the other "Five Wise Virgins" had built without men was novel, even utopian.

Privately, however, the reality was that the house was full of passionate artists who fell in and out of love with one another. Brilliant as they were, they were not immune to jealousy. Charlotte noticed when Max and Hattie started spending more time together. She saw Max's face flushed with excitement when she came home after visiting Hattie's studio. Though Charlotte claimed to be retired, it pained her to hear Max gush about

Hattie's accomplishments. Meanwhile, Charlotte spent her days socializing and writing letters. Friendship, ambition, and desire were a volatile combination.

Charlotte was hurt when Hattie began complaining that as "head of the house" Charlotte's rule over their group was becoming tyrannical. She had some cause for this. In the winter of 1854 Charlotte decided to go back to work just as Matilda Hays was rebuilding her connections to the literary world. Hattie and others discouraged Max from going with Charlotte to London, but Charlotte needed her (and privately dreaded what might happen if Max stayed home with Hattie).

When they boarded the train from Rome to London for a stay of several months, Charlotte clearly hoped the time together would help them reconcile. She'd even planned a romantic trip to Paris. But shortly after they arrived, Max changed her mind and went back to Rome and to Hattie.

"I can never suffer so much again," Charlotte later wrote to a friend about that winter. "God knows there is no need." She felt tortured. Forcing herself through the snow to rehearsal, then back to her bed, at times she even felt suicidal. She dealt with her pain as she always did, by making it into art.

She threw herself into the role of Queen Katharine, the tragic heroine of Shakespeare's *Henry VIII*. In the play, Henry abandons Katharine, his first wife, for the young, fertile Anne Boleyn. Charlotte was thirty-eight and thought she might be getting a little old to play Romeo, but felt the aging Katharine suited her perfectly. Compared to the anguish and messiness of Charlotte's private life, Katharine's pain is wonderfully pure, closer to the suffering of Charlotte's puritan ancestors. The role let Charlotte play the wronged wife, to bathe in the audience's sympathy for a woman betrayed.

She dressed for the role as if for a funeral, in black silk velvet, skillfully embroidered with gold vines that climbed her body. Invisible inside the hem was a band of extravagant hand-wrought lace, an opulent bit of perfectionism the audience would never see. The material was weighted at the hem, so that when she walked it looked like she was treading water. As she moved, her teardrop pearl earrings swung against the high ivory collar of her dress. Everything about her was pure and noble.

Reviews were rapturous, some of the best she'd ever received. In London she was celebrated by poets, painters, composers, singers—artists of all kinds. She spent her vacation in Paris with a new friend who unlike Max had an upbeat temperament, and with her two dogs: a hound named Guy and a terrier called Gyp. She also bought a fast new horse and spent her leisure time riding.

In the spring, Charlotte returned to Rome and Max came home to her, having spent a "miserable winter" without her. Charlotte was secretly thrilled at the reversal. "I believe in her suffering," Charlotte wrote to Grace. "I am proud to say that, notwithstanding what she made me suffer, I still believe in Miss Hays." Still, Charlotte had not been entirely alone in London, and Max was "very indignant to find my little friend had almost seemed to take her place. Very penitent and wretched. Having found and had the generosity to confess her mistake in having left me . . . And now that she has found her mistake, and in a short time, now, we shall be together again. Never again perhaps to be what she once was. But still perhaps better that I am not so dependent upon her and that she has tried others." They lived together for the next three years, until finally tensions erupted so publically neither could deny that it was time to end it.

It was April 1857, Charlotte was at her desk at home in Rome. She was writing a letter when Max came downstairs and demanded to know who it was addressed to. When Charlotte refused to answer, Max tried to snatch the letter from her. Charlotte ran across the room with the letter and stuffed it in her mouth rather than "give her the satisfaction." "I'll make you swallow it!" Max shouted, and chased Charlotte around the house trying to shove the note down her throat.

Hattie arrived at that moment and tried to keep them apart, but to her shock Max only cursed at her and tore away. They continued arguing "like fishwives," until Hattie left, disgusted. Two days later, Max wrestled her bags out the door into the chilly spring air and left Rome and Charlotte behind. If Charlotte thought she would come back again, she realized the finality of Max's decision when she received a note from a lawyer; Max was suing her for more than $2,000. She claimed Charlotte owed her this because she had given up her career for their relationship. Though the two women weren't legally married, Max felt she had a reasonable case and was in any event angry enough to drag Charlotte into court. Charlotte paid the amount in full, bringing the whole affair to a bitter end.

The bust-up with Matilda Hays left Charlotte feeling skittish. Their passion had threatened Charlotte's reputation as a matronly, "pure" woman who only experienced violent emotion onstage. She policed her public image to protect her private life. It was better to seem an old maid than a woman who loved other women.

When Charlotte met Emma Stebbins, it was spring in Rome and the ground was warming, the banks of the Tiber thrumming with green new growth. Americans began to flood into Rome in larger numbers, resting against boulders after the steep climb to the Colosseum and filling the streets and cafés. Women sweated and fainted under a new extreme fashion called the crinoline—a wide brass or metal hoop that extended for several feet on either side and held the waist in a vice-like grip.

Charlotte was immediately attracted to Emma's sense of self-sufficiency and the quiet, ladylike demeanor that hid a talented sculptor. Emma had grown up comfortably, the daughter of a wealthy family in Boston. Now, at forty-one (the same age as Charlotte), she was following in the footsteps of other women sculptors, like Harriet Hosmer and had moved to Rome to learn from the old masters.

Being with Emma made Charlotte feel calm and happy. Charlotte described her as a traditional woman, of noble character, high-minded and self-sacrificing. Charlotte's friends noticed she became more ladylike around Emma. Charlotte had taken to wearing men's fashions with Max, but now she emulated Emma's more conservative dress—a hoop skirt and dark colors—abandoning her tie and jacket for white lace cuffs and collar. Emma's family disliked Charlotte; they didn't like the fact that she was an actress, and they worried Emma would be morally tainted by the association. Still, it wasn't long before Emma moved into Charlotte's large new house on the Via Gregoriana.

Throughout the summer of 1857 Charlotte and Emma lived in relative domestic bliss. They woke at eight, breakfasted

*Charlotte Cushman
and Emma Stebbins*

together, then walked down the Spanish Steps to the Via del Corso, where Emma shared a studio with Hattie. Charlotte read and watched her partner work until lunchtime. She wanted to be near Emma, despite the fact that sculptors' studios were not romantic aeries but rough places with bare floors, plastered walls, a few old chairs and blocks of marble, with sketches of nude figures hanging on the whitewashed walls.

chapter thirteen

The Coming Storm

———— ◆ ◆ ————

In the fall of 1857 Charlotte again returned to America, along with Emma and Sallie. Charlotte had hired an unreliable financial manager, and she decided to go back on the road to replace some of the money she had lost. Through Hattie, whom she remained close to, she wrote to a respected St. Louis businessman named Wayman Crow, and he agreed to help manage her wealth, which was now considerable. Crow, like Charlotte, had worked his way to the top. He started his career as a young apprentice sleeping in a cot in the store-room of a dry goods store and ended up buying the store and many others like it.

Thankfully, the American public was as eager to see Charlotte Cushman as ever. Though still the minority, more women filled the seats of the theaters, and female critics amplified Charlotte's fame with long features about her in magazines and newspapers. At forty-one, Charlotte had become an idol to young women, some who found the older actress irresistibly attractive, and were eager to take part in the women's liberation movement beginning to gain momentum in America. One of them was the young writer Louisa May Alcott, who saw Charlotte perform in Boston and wrote afterward in her diary: "Saw Charlotte Cushman and had a stage-struck fit."

Another was Mary Devlin, a beautiful eighteen-year-old actress whom Charlotte hired to play Juliet opposite her Romeo in New York. Mary was a dark-haired Irish girl with a clear oval face, full lips, wide-set eyes, and a frank, somewhat wry expression. Charlotte thought she was talented, and when their New York run finished she invited Mary to come along on her tour to St. Louis.

Mary idolized Charlotte, signed her letters "your Juliet," and asked her for romantic advice. Mary had met and was falling in love with Edwin Booth, the American-born son of the British star Junius Brutus Booth and Mary Ann Holmes. The Booths were theatre royalty. Edwin's two brothers, John Wilkes and Junius Jr., were also successful actors. Mary confided in Charlotte that Edwin wanted to marry her, but had broken off the engagement because his sister Asia was against the match. Asia hated actresses and hated that Mary was Irish (which she considered low class), and thought she was a gold digger, "an actress—not even second rate . . . who can stroll before a nightly audience—who can allow men of all kinds to caress and court her in a business way."

Asia idolized her brother, but he had problems of his own.

Mary Devlin Booth

Like his father, he was an alcoholic who seduced the young women who played "utility parts," hoping for their big break. Writing to his brother Junius Jr. in California, Edwin bragged that he had a "little sweetheart" who was crazy to go to California, too, but "I talked her out of it and my p . . . k into her . . . She is a singing chambermaid. I won't mention her name—I think you know her." Six weeks later he wrote to his brother again, worried he might have the clap.

Edwin's genius and "rawness," at playing tragic figures like Othello, Shylock, and Hamlet, made him appealing both to men and women. Adam Badeau, a young critic, fell hard for Edwin and felt a "peculiar intimacy" between them. During the summer of 1858, while Booth was deciding what to do about his feelings for Mary Devlin, he invited Badeau to stay with him at Tudor Hall, his family home in Bel Air, Maryland. The house was nearly empty, and the two young men spent the night poring over Booth's playbills and costumes before falling asleep in each other's arms.

Mary knew all about Edwin's affairs, but "felt that her fate was to marry him" so, despite her reservations, Charlotte tried to be supportive. She advised Mary to start a rumor while on tour that she had another marriage proposal, which they both knew would drive Edwin mad with jealousy. It worked, and soon he was writing to Mary again. When Mary finished the tour she went back to New York and they were married.

While Charlotte traveled west, Emma Stebbins stayed behind on the East Coast with friends and family. When she arrived in St. Louis, Charlotte wrote to Wayman Crow, her financial manager, to invite him and his family to see her perform. Crow came to see her as Romeo in *Romeo and Juliet* and brought along his daughters, Emma and Cornelia. Emma Crow was disturbed and excited by Charlotte's Romeo: "never having seen it until then, Miss Cushman as Romeo seemed the incarnation of the ideal lover," she remembered a decade later, "and realized all the dreams that flitted through a girl's fancy."

In the balcony scene, Emma watched two women make love in plain sight. "At the moment of impassioned parting," she remembered, "Romeo returned again and again for a last embrace and finally pressed one of (Juliet's) ringlets to his lips."

After the performance, Wayman Crow introduced Charlotte to his family, and during the rest of her time in St. Louis, Charlotte spent all her free time with nineteen-year-old Emma. By the time Charlotte finally left Missouri, the two women were in love.

"Darling mine, I wish you would burn my letters," Charlotte wrote to Emma Crow on June 20, as she departed for Albany, New York: "You do not know into whose hands an accident might make them fall." "If you do not promise to burn them I shall have to be careful how I write and you will not like that," she warned, "You can always keep one and when another comes then destroy the old one," she advised. But Emma Crow ignored the request. And even after Charlotte returned to Rome that winter with Emma Stebbins she continued to write to her "little lover" with abandon.

Charlotte settled back into her domestic routine in Rome, but after the breakneck speed of her tour, her days seemed prosaic. She rose at 7 a.m., had breakfast with her household at 8, and then said goodbye to Emma Stebbins, who began the mile-long walk to her studio. Charlotte's friends, it seemed, were looking more ragged than before. Hattie was often out at all hours, going to parties, and their mutual friend Elizabeth Barrett Browning worried she might be taking drugs. (Elizabeth herself was addicted to opium.)

The physical pain Charlotte often felt after the rigors of performing and after the nausea of ocean travel did not retreat even after days of rest, and she often was too tired to complete even the simplest daily tasks. The weather was bad that winter, the paths too slippery and treacherous for riding. She felt stifled and ill, and the only cure seemed to be her letters from Emma Crow.

In letters to Emma Crow she now referred to her partner as "Miss Stebbins" and claimed they were only good friends. Emma Stebbins knew about the other Emma but thought it was a passing flirtation. When she found out that Charlotte was still writing to her, she was furious.

Charlotte denied that she had done anything wrong and went ahead and invited Emma Crow to Rome. As a buffer, she also invited Ned to come at the same time. Now grown-up, Ned had been working in India and had recently recovered from a long illness. In her letters to Emma Crow, Charlotte bragged about Ned's good looks, especially his new beard, which she said made him look more manly.

When Emma Crow arrived, she was hurt that Charlotte avoided her, trusting her together with Ned. Ned seemed interested, and after several weeks together he proposed. Emma married Ned and by a kind of transitive property took Charlotte's name, becoming Emma Cushman. The arrangement was meant to placate Stebbins, but it also gave Charlotte and her little lover license to spend as much time together as they wanted.

Even after the marriage, tensions in the household grew, and finally the newlyweds decided to move back to America. The move was painful for Emma Cushman, who had married Ned believing she could continue her love affair with Charlotte. When she became pregnant, Emma hoped for "a little Charlotte," and after she and Ned moved back to America, Charlotte wrote to her daily, openly wishing the unborn baby was her and Emma's child. When Emma miscarried late in her pregnancy, they were both devastated. But Emma soon became pregnant again, and when the little boy was safely delivered, Charlotte rushed across the Atlantic to be at Emma's side.

Though she was deeply wounded by the affair, Emma Stebbins was too well bred to storm off to London as Max had done. She and Charlotte remained committed to each other, and though Charlotte did occasionally return to the stage in brief, frenetic burtsts, she dedicated herself to Stebbins's career. When Stebbins was competing for a commission to make a statue of

Horace Mann for the Massachusetts State House Charlotte sent free theatre tickets to Horace and his wife, the former Mary Peabody. Emma got the commission.

Emma also began working on the statue that would be her masterpiece, *Angel of the Waters* for the Bethesda Fountain in Central Park. Emma got the commission in 1862 from her brother Henry—who was then chairman of the New York Parks Committee on Statuary. The *Angel* shares Charlotte's powerful body, her strong thighs and hips, her powerful back and shoulders. The fountain would commemorate the opening of the Croton Aqueduct, which brought clean water to New York City, and would stand at the end of the Poet's Walk in Central Park. The *Angel* holds a lily, the symbol of healing. This was particularly symbolic because by the time she began designing the statue, Emma knew that Charlotte's migraines and recurring colds were symptoms of breast cancer. Though no women were celebrated on the Poet's Walk, Emma used the opportunity to make the Bethesda Fountain a secret tribute to Charlotte.

chapter fourteen

Civil Wars

◆ ◆

I n May 1854, a Democratic senator from Illinois named Stephen A. Douglas, along with President Franklin Pierce, won passage of the Kansas-Nebraska Act, which allowed slavery to be voted on state by state. Many believed Douglas would be Pierce's successor. The act, however, angered Abraham Lincoln, who decided he would not let Douglas win without a fight. Lincoln and Douglas debated each other across the country. The debate over slavery revealed that nothing had been solved by the Compromise of 1850, and bit by bit the American people became so divided that a major conflict became inevitable, even as Lincoln assumed the presidency in March 1861.

The war began in April. The Rebel Army bombarded the

garrison at Fort Sumpter and took it over, raising the Confederate flag. Then Virginia seceded from the Union. Despite this, many people assumed the war would be over by the end of the year, even William Seward, Lincoln's newly appointed secretary of state. Seward and Charlotte were good friends, and he wrote to her in Rome that he believed the war would be short-lived, she disagreed, telling him she was buying cotton shares.

In July 1861, Charlotte came to America for a brief tour and stayed with William Seward and his family in Washington. Seward took her to the White House to introduce her to the newly elected President Lincoln. He led her to Lincoln's office on the second floor, where the President rose to greet her, lanky and in his serious black suit. He dressed like someone for whom clothes were a regrettable necessity, but his personality was warm and welcoming: "Standing beside the flag in front of his marble fireplace, tilting back in his black leather chair, Lincoln drawled his eager references to the theatre, especially Shakespeare, to plays he had seen recently when he had slipped unannounced into a box." He had not seen Charlotte onstage, but he made her promise not to retire before he had seen her in *Macbeth*, his favorite play.

After Charlotte returned to Rome, the war continued to escalate. Thousands of volunteers joined the Union and Confederate armies, including many immigrants and free black men. Few had any military training. The Union Army was defeated at the Battle of Manassas (later known as the Battle of Bull Run) on July 21. More than 4,500 men died in that battle alone, though this was just the beginning; more than half a million more would die before the war's end.

By 1863 it was clear that there was more war to come than had already passed. In Rome, Charlotte read about the war with growing fear for her American friends and her homeland, "so heart sick that I hardly know how to talk or write about it."

Determined to help, she decided to return to America to raise money for the Union Army's Sanitary Commission, an organization that provided medical equipment and support to doctors and nurses on the battlefield. She knew that the more star power she could muster the more money she could raise, so she wrote to her old friend and former costar Edwin Booth about playing opposite her in *Macbeth*. Edwin, however, was in deep mourning for his wife, Mary, who had died suddenly of pneumonia in February, leaving Edwin to raise their daughter Edwina alone. Charlotte urged Edwin to say yes to her offer and do his part nevertheless.

Edwin agreed to do it, though he tried to talk her out of doing *Macbeth*. He had a small, lithe physique and his acting style tended to be meditative, while Charlotte was often described in terms of natural disasters like a "whirlwind" or wild animals like a "python" or "pantheress." It could also be argued that the nation's mood was not right for such a dark, morally difficult play. But Charlotte had a promise to keep.

In June of 1863 she sailed for America from England on a Cunard steamer. The passengers were divided according to their Northern or Southern sympathies and during the entire voyage the two groups refused to socialize with one another. Charlotte tried to stay on deck as much as possible, pacing the boards of the ship talking with the other passengers, including a merchant named Henry Swift. Swift was a seasoned traveler who imported goods from South America. He loved the theatre, and felt his children's education would not be complete until they had seen Edwin Booth and Charlotte Cushman onstage.

After many weeks at sea, recalled Swift, a call rang out for land. Though they were still a long way off, the horizon came into view as a few pilot boats raced toward the ship. Charlotte and the other "faithful ones" commandeered the gangway, "so they would be the first to hear the news the little boats carried." The first man climbed from his boat and the crowd "gave three rousing cheers and a Tiger." (A nautical saying: Mark Twain describes a "tiger" as three cheers followed by a loud growl.) "What news?" asked Charlotte and the others, their hands on their hats, ready to throw them up if it was good. The news was bad, the confederacy had rallied and won another victory. Union supporters dropped their heads. Suddenly, according to Swift, "Miss Cushman's little foot resounded on the deck with a positive protest and she said 'I don't believe a word of it,' turned upon her heel and marched away with the tread of a Spanish Cavalier." Nearby, Swift turned to a friend and said, "Three cheers for Charlotte Cushman."

When she arrived in Washington on October 9, 1863, Charlotte again stayed with the Sewards, whose house had become a social hub of Washington society. It was a large, two-story red brick building just northeast of the Capitol, with trees that grew so thickly that you could hardly see a visitor coming up the walk. William Seward was elegant and handsome and his wife, Frances, was beautiful and intellectual. Both were committed abolitionists. Their nineteen-year-old daughter, Fanny, was as brilliant as her parents and hoped to be a writer. She was used to the comings and goings of great artists, thinkers, and politicians, but Charlotte was special. She had made a lasting impression on Fanny during her visit two years earlier. To Fanny, Charlotte was proof that an unmarried woman could be happy and successful—a model for the single life she planned to lead.

During this visit, Fanny studied every detail of Charlotte's speech and appearance and made extensive notes about her in her diary. Fanny meant these notes to be a script for her future life. When Charlotte arrived, Fanny noted that she dressed almost in a military fashion, with a "drab traveling duster" and a dress of the same fabric. Under those serious traveling clothes, she sometimes also wore a pin-striped skirt and linen pin-striped shirt, with the collar and sleeves showing beneath her dress. Fanny noticed that Charlotte was "very tall—a good deal taller than myself," and stout, with steely gray hair that tended to wave, and which she wore pulled back on the sides and rolled forward at the top. Fanny thought the style balanced Charlotte's exaggerated features, her "massive brows," "expressive" eyes, a face full of "energy & firmness." Fanny guessed Charlotte was in her mid-fifties (she was forty-seven) but seemed girlish. She had a queenly grandeur and seemed lit up from within, and despite what others said, Fanny declared her beautiful, "far more beautiful than youth or regularity of features alone could be." Charlotte's mercurial expression was difficult to capture in painting or photographs, but Fanny found her face "possesses sublimity." Intelligent, full of good humor yet deeply impressive, it was the face "of a great, true woman."

Emma Crow Cushman had been traveling with Charlotte since June, and Fanny found her friendly and intelligent, but was not smitten as she was with Charlotte. When Seward came home, Charlotte joined the men talking politics. She spoke easily of current events, observed Fanny, "with the ease and air of habit which is usually confined to men,—her views comprehensive, clear, far-sighted." The men often kept her up talking until late at night. As the hub of an enormous network of friends and acquaintances—and with a massive correspondence she kept up meticulously—Charlotte had access to excellent information, and she was not shy about connecting people she liked if she thought they could do each other good. She was also widely read, funny, engaging, and an excellent conversationalist.

President Lincoln came nearly every night to dine with Charlotte while she stayed with the Sewards in Washington. Much had changed since she met him in 1861, when they still hoped the war would be over quickly. Now, three years into the war, Lincoln, like Macbeth, was "in blood stepped in so far that should I wade no more, / Returning were as tedious as go o'er."

During her last visit, Lincoln's "ready good humor" had made her laugh so much she forgot what she wanted to say. Now, however, Lincoln's face seemed "so overspread with sadness" he resembled Shakespeare's sad clown Jacques, "translated from the forest of Arden to the capital of Illinois." Yet he lit up when he spoke on subjects that interested him, like his favorite play.

"I think nothing equals *Macbeth*," Lincoln had written to the actor James Hackett three months earlier. He preferred to read Shakespeare himself, which let him study the text the way he also studied the Bible, but he also enjoyed finding out how an actor's conception of the play differed from his own. In fact, when a congressman brought the actor John McDonough to the White House one night, Lincoln kept him talking for four hours about Shakespeare. "Lincoln was eager to know why certain scenes were left out of productions . . . He was fascinated by the different ways classic lines could be delivered," McDonough recalled. During their conversation Lincoln often lifted his "well-thumbed volume" of Shakespeare from the shelf, reading aloud some passages, reciting others from memory. Charlotte, who had seen Hackett perform in 1845 and declared him terrible, was celebrated for her understanding of the sense as well as the effect of Shakespeare's lines. Lincoln was eager to see her and had tickets for the night of October 17.

A few days before the performance, Charlotte and Fanny took a tour of the new Ford's Theatre. The theatre was only a few blocks away, on Tenth Street, so they walked, talking animatedly the whole way. Inside Ford's Theatre daylight streamed in through the high windows. In a nod to growing female audiences, the building had a separate ladies' entrance and exit. Charlotte entertained Fanny by revealing stage secrets. Next to the prompter's box was a long, hollow piece of iron filled with dried peas hung on the wall. Charlotte took hold of it and shook it mightily, making thunder.

On the night of October 17 Lincoln walked to Grover's Theatre, a few blocks from the Capitol and within spitting distance of Ford's, its rival. Grover's was not well insulated, and was known to be cold in winter and hot in summer, but Lincoln had been there more than a hundred times, sometimes with Seward, sometimes alone. "Exceedingly conversant in Shakespeare," Lincoln turned to the Bard to help him in a time of great stress. As with the Bible, Shakespeare gives no straightforward answers, but riddles, which, when puzzled out, offered a method for thinking through a problem.

Macbeth begins on a battlefield, the war already lost and won. It is a play not about war but what comes after, themes already on the President's mind: "o'er-leaping ambition" that jumps over the top step and falls on the other side. Ambition is, as in the Bible, an "illness" rather than a virtue (a profoundly un-American sentiment). Ambition makes Macbeth paranoid and makes Lady Macbeth mad.

That freezing October night the dead still lay unburied on the field at Gettysburg, where they had been rotting since July. On Lindon's desk lay an unfinished draft of the Gettysburg Address.

In the icy auditorium, Lincoln watched Charlotte as Lady Macbeth in the sleep-walking scene. She seemed to glide downstage silently as a ghost, violently wringing her hands, trying to wash away the unseen gore: "Out, damned spot! out, I say!—One: two: why, then, 'tis time to do't.—Hell is murky!—Fie, my lord, fie! a soldier, and afeard?"

The scene echoes the Old Testament's Matthew 27:24, where Pontius Pilate washes Jesus's blood from his hands. With his long study of Shakespeare and the Bible, Lincoln would have recognized the way the Bard associates Lady Macbeth and her husband with Pilate the traitor. He may also have recalled Pilate's next lines: "I am innocent of this man's blood," Pilate announces. "You shall bear the responsibility." And the people answer, "His blood be on us and on our children!"

A year later, in 1864, Edwin Booth and his brothers, Junius Jr. and John Wilkes, performed together at the Winter Garden in New York, in a benefit production of *Julius Caesar*. The event raised more than $5,000 to fund a statue of William Shakespeare for Central Park.

John Wilkes Booth thought he saw a message in the play. Though he played Marc Antony, he saw himself as an avenging Brutus murdering the tyrant Caesar and restoring the republic. It was a role that would eventually consume him, and on the night of April 14, 1865, he shot Lincoln from behind on the balcony of Ford's Theatre. Then he jumped onstage waving a gun crying out "*sic semper tyrannis,*" an echo of what Brutus is thought to have shouted as he murdered Caesar. *Thus always to tyrants.* In the balcony the President slumped in his chair, a bullet in his head. Nine hours later, the great emancipator was dead.

By the time Charlotte heard the news in Rome, it was a week later. She was horrified. She had known and worked with John Wilkes Booth, and disliked him intensely, calling him reckless, drunken, a "dare-devil." Her grief for Lincoln was profound. His death made her feel how far away she was, and "brought the war home" to her. "My heart feels as if it was cramped in a vise," she wrote, circling again and again back to the tragedy, in anger and disbelief; it was everywhere.

She also worried about Edwin Booth and his daughter, Edwina. They were hiding out in a hotel room in New York. Edwin was afraid they would be killed by a mob if they left, anticipating that his brother's crime would attach itself to him and his family "forever and forever!" Drinking heavily and suicidal, Edwin seemed only to want to disappear. But friends convinced him to speak out publicly against his brother's actions. Finally, he published a letter on behalf of the rest of the Booth family, declaring their loyalty to the Union and grief over Lincoln's death, which went some way toward appeasing the mob.

After the assasination, John Wilkes Booth had fled the theatre, hiding with other conspirators on a farm outside Virginia. On April 26, 1865, he was captured and killed by government troops. A doctor was called to identify the body, and he lifted the traitor's head to look on the back of his neck. As a teenager, this doctor had been assisting in his father's surgery when John Wilkes Booth came in for an operation to remove a fibroid tumor in his neck. But after the operation the wound was reopened and healed badly, leaving a long scar that looked like a burn. The doctor reported that it had been Charlotte Cushman who had accidentally ripped open the would during a violent onstage embrace.

As the nation quickly realized, the assasination had been part of a broader conspiracy. Members of the same group had also attacked William Seward and other members of the cabinet, trying to destabilize the government. Young Fred Seward bravely fought off the assassin sent to kill his father but was badly injured in the attack. He survived his injuries, but Mrs. Seward never recovered from her terror and died weeks after the conspirators were hanged. Charlotte was "much broken down with anxiety" about Seward and his family and was further devastated when, a year later, young Fanny died of tuberculosis.

In her anger and grief over the assault on her government, Charlotte composed an open letter on behalf of American ex- patriates in Italy, which she presented at a memorial to Lin- coln at the American Legation in Rome: "We have heard with mingled emotions of horror and regret too deep for utterance, the appalling intelligence of the cruel and cowardly attack," she wrote. "In common with every true-hearted American, at home and abroad, we regard the loss of Abraham Lincoln as a national bereavement of unsurpassed magnitude."

Lincoln's death, and the subsequent end of the war in April 1865, made Charlotte wish she were closer to home, to share her country's grief and recovery. She was also feeling physically sick again, like a "worn out broken wrinkled lunatic." "I think," she wrote to her friend Helen Hunt, "I may perhaps be carrying my own death warrant. Yet, after all, who does not."

Charlotte's homesickness finally overwhelmed her when, in 1869 she was diagnosed with breast cancer. Charlotte decided that aggressive surgery was the best option and Emma Stebbins took time away from her work to care for her. The press reported on her illness and surgeries with morbid curiosity. Her surgeon was the famous Scottish doctor Sir James Simpson, who had pioneered the use of chloroform for anesthesia. But during the lumpectomy to remove tumors in her breasts, Charlotte refused anesthetic. She was not being brave; she had been researching her condition in medical journals and learned that although chlo- roform was the drug of choice—even used on Queen Victoria during the birth of Prince Leopold—it could have lethal side effects.

Although the surgery seemed successful at first, the tumors came back. Charlotte did not lose hope and kept up-to-date on the latest treatments, reading medical journals in German that friends in the field sent to her. She wrote to her doctor asking about a new herbal remedy using the bark of a tree, which had only just been discovered in Ecuador, and wrote to the secretary of state in America asking him to put her in touch with the Ecuadorian ambassador.

Though she scaled back to be Charlotte's caregiver, Emma Stebbins continued working on *The Angel of the Waters*. It would celebrate the completion of the Croton Aqueduct, which would bring clean drinking water to much of the city. The *Angel*— which Emma modeled after Charlotte—symbolized health and healing.

The era of the Jolly Bachelors had ended with the war, and Charlotte dreamed of a home in American big enough for Ned and Emma Cushman's children. "Newport is the place to live," Charlotte wrote to a close friend. "New York to work and Boston, if you are independent and impudent, to know your heart in." After the war, Newport became a destination for New York intellectuals and artists, but also for inventors, scientists, educators, and city planners. Residents included Julia Ward Howe, Henry and William James, Oliver Wendell Holmes, John Singer Sargent, Henry Wadsworth Longfellow, Edwin Booth, and many others. Charlotte asked her friend Thomas Wentworth Higginson, who had a house in Newport, to find her a house big enough for her; Emma Stebbins and her sister; Ned and Emma Cushman and their children; and a rotating cast of friends. With Charlotte's wealth and connections it wasn't hard to find one. They called the new house Villa Cushman.

chapter fifteen

Villa Cushman

◆ ◆

In Winslow Homer's etching *The Bathe at Newport*, the water rises to eye level. The bathers soak up to their necks in the calm water. A man with brilliantined hair and a handlebar mustache splashes a woman in an elegant bathing costume floating on her back. Bodies seem to connect underwater. It's a somewhat cartoonish depiction of the Newport bathing glitterati, but it captured the decadence and sensuality of the seaside paradise, which with Saratoga in Upstate New York was one of America's first two resort towns, entirely devoted to pleasure and leisure.

A few hours up the coast from New York City, Newport offered quiet, natural beauty, and the healing sea air. Some, like Washington Irving, found it "too gay and fashionable" with

163

The Bathe at Newport *by Winslow Homer*

its dance halls and expensive restaurants and flocks of summer beachgoers, but Charlotte agreed with Henry James, whose favorite thing to do in Newport was "Nursing a nostalgia on the sun-warmed rocks."

The "Villa Cushman" was completed in 1872 and Charlotte and Emma immediately moved in full-time. It was expansive and expensive, with a large, wraparound porch from which Charlotte had a view of "my sea and my sunsets." Windows on three levels faced the water, and there were enough bedrooms to host the whole Cushman family when they came for the summer. The children were Charlotte's greatest joy. They were "very well & happy," and when they came to visit they brought her "little offerings" until their small, magical gifts and flowers "surrounded me on every side."

But when the high season ended and the children left, Charlotte's depression returned. To remedy the situation, Emma

Stebbins's sister, Mrs. Garland, moved in with them temporarily. Charlotte found her a "timid, shy, proud person"with "a sweet poetic mind" and liked her very much. Charlotte also wrote to several friends, including the novelist Helen Hunt, inviting them to come stay in the house. Also born and bred in Massachusetts, Hunt was an activist who wrote frequently about the treatment of Native Americans in the United States. She was also an advocate of other writers, corresponding frequently with Emily Dickinson and encouraging her to publish her poems: "It is cruel and wrong to your 'day & generation,'" Helen would write to Emily in 1884, "that you will not give them light." Charlotte encouraged Helen to keep writing, even after her latest collection of poetry was panned by the critics. "I don't believe any of our American men know how to criticize your poems," Charlotte wrote, "because they are so full of feeling."

Charlotte hoped to recreate at the Villa Cushman what she'd had in Rome: a gathering of writers, artists, and family, knit together under one roof and watched over by her and Emma Stebbins. But the relationship had never recovered from Charlotte's continuing passion for Emma Crow Cushman. When Helen Hunt called Emma Stebbins Charlotte's wife, Charlotte corrected her. "You are wrong dear in your term 'wife Emma,'" she confided, explaining that she and Stebbins had not been more than friends since the arrival of Emma Crow Cushman, "the gentlemanly little person of whom we have spoken."

Still, Charlotte was happier in Newport than she had been in many years, until one day when she woke feeling chilled, then had attacks of fever. With despair she felt again a hard mass growing in her breast and knew she would likely need another operation. Sickness made the demands of daily life seem suffo-cating, the "immediate present seized, held, grabbed, clutched, clawed, demanded, asked, begged, entreated & coaxed" her until she no longer felt "mistress of my soul." She felt she was wasting the little time she had left, and that her intellect was declining without use. "Can't even hold my pen straight enough to spell correctly & a disordered stomach & weak driveling ideas!"

Rest seemed to have helped for a time, but it was no com-plete cure. The only thing Charlotte felt she could do was to go back to work. Though she was too weak to stand for an entire performance, she could still give an excellent dramatic reading, leaning on a podium or sitting in a chair. Even after all this time, she had not lost her talent for oration and capturing an audience's imagination. Her magnificently harrowed voice made a garden appear where only the bare ground of the stage once stood. "I won't give up reading, Ever, while life lasts!" she swore, though she often had to perform with a doctor waiting in the wings.

Audiences rewarded her return to the stage with excitement and passion. Many of the older patrons remembered Char-lotte from their youth, and connected her career with some of the most memorable and happy times of their lives. Everything now was divided into before and after the war, and Charlotte reminded them of a simpler time.

"When I wish to be antediluvian," wrote Henry James, "I live over a small incident of childhood, very young childhood." He was referring to a cold, dark winter night when he had sat with his brother William alone at home, their heads bent over a book, a lamp held between them. Their parents were out at the theatre, watching Charlotte Cushman in *Henry VIII* at the Park Theatre. Mr. and Mrs. James were so moved by Charlotte's performance, they rushed "from the far down town" during an intermission and retrieved William so he could catch the remainder of Charlotte's performance. Henry was left alone in a small pool of light to read while his brother experienced a "sudden infinite widening of this little lamplit circle, to soul and sense."

Seeing Charlotte perform was like being dipped in consciousness. It was a rite of passage.

Years later, James bought a ticket to see one of Charlotte's staged readings. He initially thought she looked sickly. Yet even weakened by cancer, sitting alone in a chair, her magnetism reached out to him. As she read from *Henry VIII*, her frailty added realistic pathos to her portrayal of the weakened Queen Katharine. When he left the theatre, he was stirred. It was "one of the most ineffaceable in my tolerably rich experience of the theatre . . . a vivid vigil in which the poor lonely lamplight became that of the glittering stage, in which I saw wonderous figures and listened to thrilling tones, in which I knew 'Shakespeare acted' as I was never to know him again."

Far from being a pale imitation of the play, Charlotte's voice did as much to fill a theatre as a whole troupe of actors. Thomas Wentworth Higginson discovered that just by listening to Charlotte recite a poem he could "see every fibre of thatch on the roof and every bristle on the dog's back." The critic George T. Ferris called her a "magician," bringing Shakespeare's characters back to life: "She has but to wave her wand to unlock from the prison-house of Shakespeare's pages all the immortal phantoms that brood within them," Ferris wrote. "It is for her alone to invest them with a splendid and subtle life." Now in her sixties, Charlotte was helpless to stop the illness that was clawing its way into her. But she could, if only for an hour, wake Shakespeare from the dead.

chapter sixteen

Contrary Winds

◆ ◆

The cold February air brought the smell of the sea beyond Long Wharf. "Twice a day," wrote Emerson, "the flowing sea took Boston in its arms." It was 1876 and Charlotte had returned home to Boston for medical treatment. She left the opulent downtown Parker House, where she and Emma Stebbins were staying, and walked by herself through the city where she had spent her childhood. During her walk, Charlotte caught a cold. The next day she stayed in bed, shivering and feverish. Her cold quickly turned into pneumonia, known at the time as the "captain of the men of death." As Emma Stebbins brought her medicines and warm drinks, she could hear a storm starting up outside the window.

Blocks away, the Great Elm on Boston Common thrashed in the winds. In its trunk was a hole "big enough for a nine-year-old boy to hide in," and despite its immensity, inside it was rotten. The Great Elm was more than two hundred years old, and the city had grown up around it. When the storm finally stopped, a crowd of people gathered in the Common, standing around the corpse of the great, fallen tree.

Ned and Emma Cushman arrived to help, and Sallie never left Charlotte's side. For a day or so she seemed to recover, but the chills and fever came back raging the next morning with a strange trembling the doctor called "rigor." She coughed constantly, and faded in and out of sleep and fever dreams:

She was twenty-nine, wandering among gravestones, new to London, far from her family and the girl whose ring she wore, and miserably homesick. She was composing a poem called "The Place of Graves." The theme was mortality and the ephemerality of fame. She was on the cusp of such fame, which seemed still a "vanity" and "feverish dream."

Then, she was a little girl on her mother's lap.

Then, she was playing with Ned and Emma's children, her children, and they ran and put their arms around her, kissing her on the lips. Only God knew how much she loved them.

In Charlotte's rooms in the Parker House the doctor took Emma Stebbins to the side. He spoke gravely to her and she ran out of the room crying.

Ned brought Charlotte a glass of milk punch. It reminded Charlotte of a story she'd read by Mark Twain in the last issue of the *Atlantic Monthly*.

In 1875, the new Harlem line of the New York streetcar had

opened, and instructions for the conductor were posted on the wall, in sight of the train riders. The words were oddly rhythmic, and Noah Brooks and Isaac Bromley, two newspapermen who were riding the Fourth Avenue line and couldn't get the words out of their heads. They published the instructions as a poem, which then got stuck in Mark Twain's head. He then wrote a story called "A Literary Nightmare"—to get it out:

> *Conductor, when you receive a fare,*
> *Punch in the presence of the passenjare!*
> *A blue trip slip for an eight-cent fare,*
> *A buff trip slip for a six-cent fare,*
> *A pink trip slip for a three-cent fare,*
> *Punch in the presence of the passenjare!*
> *Chorus.*
> *Punch brothers! Punch with care!*
> *Punch in the presence of the passenjare.*

If the *Tribune* poem tormented a few hundred readers, Twain's story reached thousands. It told of a literary infection that torments a writer until a friend, who he infects, keeps bursting out in snatches of "Punch brothers! Punch with care!" in the middle of a funeral.

Back in Parker House, Ned helped Charlotte sit up to take the drink. "Come auntie," he cajoled, "here's your milk punch." Smiling, Charlotte recited: "Punch, brothers! Punch with care!" And then she fell asleep.

On February 18, 1876, one hundred years after the birth of the United States, its greatest actress, Charlotte Cushman, died. She was fifty-nine years old.

On the day of her funeral, her body lay in state in the Parker House. Hundreds of friends, family, and theatre colleagues came to pay their respects. There were so many flowers delivered that the room was transformed into a bower fit for a fairy queen.

Mourners waiting to be admitted lined up along Tremont Street, the crowd stretching past the Commons, where men groaned over the hundred-foot branches of the Great Elm, sawing them down to size.

After the viewing, the body was brought to King's Chapel for the funeral service. Family, intimate friends, and colleagues sat in the wooden pews facing the coffin while the public found whatever space they could in the galleries above. Many who had bought tickets could not get in, and the street outside grew so packed no one could get in or out. Police were stationed around the church. Charlotte's body had not been carried by train around the country, as Lincoln's had been, but her death cast the whole nation into mourning. Thousands of people came to Boston from across the country for the funeral, waiting in line for hours just to get a glimpse of her coffin.

Inside the chapel, young girls from the Cushman School, recently renamed in Charlotte's honor, walked solemnly down the long aisle between the pews. Against their white dresses they wore black sashes, and each girl carried a small bouquet of fresh flowers, which she laid inside Charlotte's open casket before taking her seat.

The chapel was "profusely ornamented" and scented with flowers, which like the dignitaries filled "every available space."

A large cross made of ivy sat on the altar, surrounded by white floral stars made of creamy, sweet-smelling camelias, lilies, white lilacs, and tea roses. Maidenhair ferns drooped among rosebuds, violets, heliotrope, and "rare orchids."

Reporters from around the world, from the *San Francisco Chronicle* to the *Irish Times*, were in attendance. They made notes as the coffin was carried out and placed into a carriage that slowly led a long and winding procession up the slope of Mount Auburn. It was a scene to rival the finest Greek drama. "We find little difference," said one pastor who included Charlotte in his sermon that Sunday, between "the true aim of both actor and preacher."

The public spectacle of Charlotte's Boston funeral was only the beginning of the national mourning that followed her death. In New York, nearly ten thousand people gathered in the streets for a candlelight vigil. It would have been difficult to find a newspaper that did not carry her obituary. All repeated the up-from-her-bootstraps story of a difficult childhood, a failure in New Orleans, and a remarkable success in London. Charlotte was compared to the best male actors of her age, and more than once to Beethoven.

She was even compared to Napoleon: "Thus we see that Charlotte Cushman did something more than walk upon the stage with a fine talent, and turn the world upside down at once. She did, indeed, what Napoleon did on another scale; she conquered circumstance; and she did it with laborious effort and indomitable will," declared *Harper's Bazaar.* "There was hardly a hearthstone among the English-speaking families of the world," wrote one reporter, "where her name was not a household word."

In life she had been famous, but in death she became a myth, one of the "Titanic beings, capable of lifting the drama to the place it held when in the old Greek amphitheaters beside the sea no roof intervened between the players and the sky above them," as *Harper's Bazaar* put it in a feature, published a month after her death, on March 18, 1876. Onstage, the writer explained, she had merged seamlessly with her characters, and in memory she fused with them entirely, making them "new beings." She even usurped the authors of the plays themselves. Charles Dickens's character Nancy was remembered as "the character [Cushman] made famous," while "her Meg Merrilies was something beyond the wild woman of Walter Scott's imagining. The indignation and defiance and pathos of her Queen Katharine made a magnificent apparition that escapes us when simply reading Shakespeare at home."

In mourning Charlotte Cushman, America also mourned its youth, forever obscured behind the fog of war: "To see her Romeo was to see the height of love and youth and joy, the very apotheosis of tragic loss at last, that made old veins tremble with the impulse of young blood spinning through them, as if it were night and summer and youth in Italian gardens and under Italian skies."

"Into a face that every man called ugly," the *Harper's Bazaar* feature continued, "she gathered a divine sweetness and strength that every woman called beauty." Her life was held up as a model for women across the world. Her success had been "snatched from the fate that has brought women so little . . . something silencing to the vast defamatory tongue that declares women of so small purpose." Charlotte's career had proved them all wrong. Since she was a girl, she had been confident of her larger purpose, and when she failed she drove herself forward anyway, creating a life of daring adventure.

epilogue

◆ ◆

Culture is not a fixed condition,
it is the unremitting interaction
between the past and the present.

—*Lawrence Levine*

But even as Charlotte was being eulogized, she was being forgotten. The late nineteenth century had been a decade of steady progress for women, including legal protections for married women, programs to keep poor women out of prostitution, and new women-only universities, but these advances had created a backlash among socially conservative critics in America and Victorian England.

To these critics, Charlotte's life was useful only as a morality tale, edited to show the most convenient and teachable moments. Many Victorian writers expressed surprise that she had been so successful despite her "plainness" and her "manly" appearance. Actors with whom she had competed for men's roles wrote in relief that women would no longer "push us from our seats." Shortly after Charlotte's death, her former friend George Vandenhoff wrote that she was "neither man-woman nor woman-man," but something unnatural and "epicene." Another obituary said that while Miss Cushman was a fine actress, American culture had so advanced that women no longer had to sully themselves by playing men onstage. When Horace Howard Furness published the definitive *New Variorum* of *Macbeth*, an anthology of writing by and about prominent actors associated with the play, he did not mention Charlotte Cushman once. Despite living for most of her life around sculptors, no public statue of Charlotte was ever commissioned. But the people who had seen her perform never forgot, and wrote in their own memoirs about the night they saw Charlotte Cushman as Romeo, Lady Macbeth, Meg, Nancy, Queen Katharine, or Hamlet. Then, for a time, she disappeared.

After Charlotte's death, the American public turned away from Shakespeare. Charlotte's genius made Shakespeare come alive for her audience, but on her death critics doubted "whether any amount of histrionic art or genius [would] be sufficient to keep Shakespeare always on the stage." Americans were more focused on work and individual success. They worked longer hours and were more exhausted during their leisure time. They wanted entertainment that asked less of them. Shakespeare gradually receded, "from congregated crowds to solitary and individual readers; more and more he becomes to thoughtful minds the POET and less and less the PLAYER." The winged communication made possible by the telegraph and popular presses also provided new opportunities for entertainment and distraction, while industrialization and longer workweeks meant less time to cram that entertainment into. Before long, Americans were more likely to encounter the Bard at a university than in the theatre.

For nearly a century, the trend toward reading rather than performing Shakespeare continued, doing no good to Shakespeare, who became associated with high culture and was avoided as a difficult text. Once a popular entertainment, now Shakespeare became canonized, and academics could make a living providing an exegesis of his work, making Shakespeare scholars into a kind of priesthood.

But somewhere around the 1960s the trend began to reverse. Shakespeare festivals began to proliferate across the country. Many were free, and all offered affordable ways for working-class Americans to see Shakespeare onstage. Americans have always been Shakespearean, and Shakespeare came to America in the first settlers' saddlebags. The love affair was rekindled, and by the 400th anniversary of the Bard's birth there were more Shakespeare festivals in America than anywhere else in the world.

Charlotte's legacy is present, though invisible, in every one of these performances. She was the first to prove that an American could interpret Shakespeare onstage. She resurrected the original text of *Romeo and Juliet*, and her interpretations of many of

Shakespeare's characters survive today. She inspired generations of women to wear the breeches, on- and offstage.

It's springtime in New York, and the *Angel's* wings are covered in dogwood blooms. Swan boats float by on the lake, while tourists underdressed for the chill take photographs of themselves standing in front of *The Angel of the Waters*. The Bethesda Fountain was unveiled in the spring of 1873 in front of a large crowd. Some critics complained the *Angel* did not look womanly enough, her strong thighs and broad shoulders making her look like a servant girl "jumping over stepping stones," with "a distinctly male head," others found the overall impression a confusing mix of male and female. But the audience adored the statue, as they had its inspiration. It remains a secret memorial to the Greatest American Actress.

Acknowledgments

Thank you to my parents, Niko and Michael, for their inspiration, love, and support and for giving me early access to art of all kinds, including taking me to Shakespeare festivals from a young age. Thank you to my sister, Carla, a true artist and my first friend. To other courageous women in my family: my grandmothers, Sarah and Signe; my aunts, Ann and Annie. My love, Alexander Landfair, for being married to this book as well as to me, and for being a caring partner and coparent who moved mountains (and toddlers) so I could have time to write. My son, Rowan, for his humor, sensitivity, and hunger for stories. My family-in-law Barbara, James, and David Landfair and Matt Taylor-Gross. My dear friends and writing companions Rachel Riederer, Meaghan Winter, Abigail Rabinowitz, Maggie Sowell, Julie Cohen, and Belinda Mckeon for their wisdom, levity, and encouragement. Thank you to my wonderful agent, Kiele Raymond, and amazing editor, Julianna Haubner, for believing in Charlotte. Thank you also to the team at Avid Reader, in particular Alexandra Pirimani, Allie Lawrence, and Morgan Hoit.

Acknowledgments

Thank you to Nicole Wallack, Sue Mendelsohn, Kristine Dahl, Patricia O'Toole, Aaron Ritzenberg, Glenn Gordon, and Bridget Potter for their friendship and generosity; their ongoing support and advice have been essential to this book. Thank you to Stacy Shiff, Margo Jefferson, Richard Locke, Arthur Phillips, Katherine Rowland, Amy Brady, Joel Whitney, Michael Archer, and the late Michael Janeway. To James Shapiro for many conversations about American Shakespeare and for being an early supporter of this book. To Jane Ackermann for excellent research assistance and providing loving childcare so I could bang my head against this manuscript. Thank you to the amazing people at *Tin House* who have nurtured so many writers: Holly MacArthur, Rob Spillman, Elissa Schappell, Michelle Wildgen, Win McCormack, and others. Thank you also to Andi Winette at *The Believer*, Michelle Legro at *Lapham's Quarterly*, Michael Knight at the Helene Wurlitzer Foundation, and the Global Scholars Institute at NYU.

Thank you to my *Guernica* family and to my colleagues at Columbia and NYU. To my teachers in and out of school: Art Lande, Jack Collum, Isolde Stewart, Kay Cook, Doug Berger, Stephen Weeks, Mike Parker, and John Zola. Thank you to my students, who have so many stories of their own to tell.

To Amy Thomas, Jennifer Heath, EJ Meade, and Frank and Viki Solomon for opening their homes to me during the writing of this book. To Paul Prescott and Paul Edmondson at the Shakespeare Birthplace Trust for inviting me along on their Great American Shakespeare Road Trip. The following people helped during critical stages in the research process: Matthew Wittmann at Harvard's Houghton Theatre Library, Meghan

180

Acknowledgments

Carafano at the Folger Shakespeare Library, Jennifer Lee at Columbia University's rare books and manuscripts division, Kenneth Cohen at the Smithsonian National Museum for American History, the librarians at the Schlesinger Library, Alexander Nemerov, Tom Bogar, Faye Charpentier, Barbara Wallace Grossman, Robin Rausch, and many, many others.

Notes on Sources

The Charlotte Cushman papers in the Library of Congress contain thousands of letters and many of Cushman's personal scrapbooks; even bad notices were preserved with care. That these letters survive is remarkable. Cushman, like many nineteenth-century luminaries, preferred to keep her public and private lives separate and consigned most of her personal correspondence to the fire. But her lover of many years and later daughter-in-law, Emma Crow, ignored Cushman's repeated requests to "burn this letter." It is thanks to Crow's loving rebellion that we have this wealth of material on one of the greatest American actresses. This period is explored in detail in Lisa Merrill's book *When Romeo Was a Woman: Charlotte Cushman and Her Circle of Female Spectators*. Thank you in particular to Walter Zvonchenko at the Library of Congress. The work of Lawrence Levine was especially transformative, as was the work of Bruce McConachie.

Materials that speak to Cushman as an artist—her goals, methods, the high and low points of her career, what she meant to her audiences—are scattered across the country and across the globe. The Folger Shakespeare Library houses several of Cushman's original playbills, as well as letters and reviews that help establish her as a prime mover in America's love affair with Shakespeare. The Houghton Theatre Library at Harvard was essential in reconstructing Cushman's nineteenth-century context. Their archives also hold letters to Cushman from Henry Wadsworth Longfellow about a play he wanted to write for her, and theatrical ephemera including the "Macready dagger." Smithsonian curator Kenneth Cohen's article "The Woman Who Would Be Cardinal" alerted me to the existence of several of Cushman's original costumes in the Smithsonian National Museum of American History. These costumes, one of which was once preserved in arsenic, gave me a valuable glimpse of Cushman onstage. The Annie Fields papers at the Massachusetts Historical Society and Harriet Hosmer papers at the Schlesinger Library helped illuminate Cushman's friendships with other women artists.

Columbia University's rare books and manuscripts division at Butler Library preserves Cushman's only extant diary, a tiny, pocket-size journal bound in red leather. The Morgan Library archives contain correspondence between Charles Dickens and William Macready about Cushman. The Thomas Sully journals at the New York Public Library rare books and manuscripts division helped fill in details about Cushman's life with Rosalie Sully's family.

The New England Historical society kindly provided copies of their Cushman letters as did the National Library of Scotland. The New York Historical Society houses letters from Cushman's early years, and the New York Public Library for the Performing

Arts is a treasure trove of material on New York theatre and contains reviews of Cushman's roles not found elsewhere. The *Brooklyn Daily Eagle* digital archives were useful in locating Walt Whitman's early reviews of Cushman. The Seward House Museum generously shared material about Cushman found in Fanny Seward's diary. Jessy Randall at Colorado College was a great help in pointing me to and sharing the papers of Helen Hunt Jackson and the many letters between Jackson and Cushman in the archive.

In New Orleans, I discovered that the site of the St. Charles Theatre is now a Marriott, but maps of nineteenth-century New Orleans digitized by the Louisiana Historical Society made it possible to piece together the city as Cushman knew it. In Boston, Cushman's residences no longer stand, but you can find tours that will lead you through her old stomping grounds. In New York, the Bowery and Park Theatres are long gone, but the lively theatrical culture they inspired remains. A fellowship from New York University's Global Research Initiative supported research in Italy, which filled in important details about the female artist colony Cushman helped create in Rome.

prologue

1   *"She is the rage"*: George C. Foster, *New York by Gaslight and Other Urban Sketches* (California: University of California Press, 1990), 151.

2   *An enormous crystal chandelier*: *The Cambridge Guide to American Theatre*, Eds. Don B. Wilmeth and Tice L. Miller (Cambridge, UK: Cambridge University Press, 1996).

2 *"American Queen of Tragedy"*: "Charlotte Cushman," *New York Herald*, November 21, 1874.

3 *"Shakespeare!"*: Richard Henry Stoddard, *The Poems of Richard Henry Stoddard* (Ann Arbor, Michigan: University of Michigan Library, 2005), 405.

4 *"our Charlotte"*: Foster, *New York By Gaslight*, 149.

4 *"I was, by a press of circumstances"*: William Thompson Price, *A Life of Charlotte Cushman* (New York: Brentano's, 1894), 169.

6 *"take me quickly at any moment"*: Clara Erskine Clement Waters, *Charlotte Cushman* (Boston, Massachusetts: James R. Osgood and Company, 1882), 105.

6 *"rockets set up all the way"*: Emma Stebbins, *Charlotte Cushman: Her Letters and Memories of Her Life* (Boston, Massachusetts: James R. Osgood and Company, 1879), 265.

7 *"What is or can be the record of an actress"*: Ibid., 11.

7 *"towering grandeur of her genius"*: Walt Whitman, "About Acting," *Brooklyn Daily Eagle*, August 14, 1846.

7 *"Saw Charlotte Cushman and had a stage-struck fit"*: Louisa May Alcott, *Louisa May Alcott: Her Life, Letters and Journals* (Boston, Massachusetts: Roberts Brothers, 1892), 99.

8 *"that these dead shall not have died in vain"*: Abraham Lincoln, "Gettysburg Address," Nicolay copy, Library of Congress, 1863.

8 *"incarnate power"*: William Winter, *Other Days* (New York: Moffat, Yard and Company, 1908), 152–53, quoted in Sharon Marcus, *The Drama of Celebrity* (Princeton, NJ: Princeton University Press, 2019), 45.

Notes on Sources

chaper one: The First Disaster

9 *"The effect of democracy"*: Alexis de Toqueville, *Democracy in America: Complete and Unabridged Volumes I and II* (New York: Random House, 2004), 752, originally published in 1835.

9 *America was considered a "vulgar" nation*: Ibid., 183. He calls Americans vulgar no less than thirteen times. Also see Fanny Trollope, *Domestic Manners of the Americans* (1832); Charles Dickens, *American Notes* (1850). Also Simon Linguet (1780) quoted in Barry Rubin and Judith Kolp Rubin, *Hating America, A History* (London: Oxford University Press, 2004), 23.

11 *"a good singer, a good scholar"*: Henry Wyles Cushman, "Genealogy of the Cushmans," Library of Congress, Charlotte Cushman Papers.

12 *"The seasons turned backward"*: *Vermont, a Guide to the Green Mountain State* (Boston: Houghton Mifflin, 1931), written by workers of the Federal Writers' Project, Works Progress Administration for the State of Vermont, 31.

12 *some argued the crisis was caused by deforestation* http:// www.newenglandhistoricalsociety.com/john-l-sullivan -americas-first-superstar-athlete/.

12 *"our philosophy e'er dreamt on"*: Quoted in *The Reporter* (Brattleboro, VT), July 17, 1816, six days before Charlotte Cushman's birth.

13 *"Climbing trees was an absolute passion"*: Stebbins, *Charlotte Cushman*, 13.

14 *"tomboy"*: Ibid.

15 *"child-brother"*: Ibid., 183.

15 *"keener, more artistic, more impulsive"*: Stebbins, *Charlotte Cushman*, 183.

15 *"tyrannical" to her siblings*: Ibid, 14.

17 *"first disaster"*: Charlotte Cushman to Emma Crow Cushman, Rome, May 21, 1861, Library of Congress, Charlotte Cushman Papers.

19 *nervous exhaustion*: "The Influence of Railway Traveling on Public Health," *Lancet*, January 4, 1862.

chapter two: Quest

21 *"that dark, horrible, guilty 'third tier'"*: Claudia D. Johnson, "That Guilty Third Tier: Prostitution in Nineteenth-Century American Theaters," *American Quarterly* 27, no. 5, Special Issue: Victorian Culture in America (December 1975): 575–84.

22 *"Pastors, deacons, church members"*: Charles Upham, *Salem Witchcraft, Volumes I and II* (New York: Frederick Ungar Publishing Co., 1867).

24 *"assumed the actors must be depraved"*: Meredith Bartron, "The Tenter-Hooks of Temptation: The Debate over Theatre in Post-Revolutionary America," *Gettysburg Historical Journal* 2, article 8 (2003).

24 *The theatre's marble facade shone creamy white*: Phillip Harry, *Tremont Theatre 1843* (Painting), Oil on Panel, 34.92 x 40.96 cm, Museum of Fine Arts, Boston.

26 *"seemed a man of quick, irritable feelings"*: Frances

Williams-Wynn, *Diaries of a Lady of Quality* (London: Longman Green, Longman, Roberts and Green, 1864), 288.

26 *families in the pit*: Lawrence Levine, *Highbrow / Lowbrow: The Emergence of Cultural Hierarchy in America* (Cambridge, Mass.: Harvard University Press). Copyright © 1988 by the President and Fellows of Harvard College.

26 *The ladies glinted like constellations*: Charlotte Cushman to Unknown, Walnut St. Theatre, January 1, 1842, Library of Congress, Charlotte Cushman Papers.

30 *Throughout Charlotte's audition Mrs. Wood was quiet*: Stebbins, *Charlotte Cushman*, 20.

30 *"that such a voice, properly cultivated"*: Ibid.

chapter three: Transformation

33 *The water of the Mississippi*: Walt Whitman, "Sailing the Mississippi at Midnight," *New Orleans Daily Crescent*, March 6, 1848.

34 *"the dwellings would speedily disappear"*: Francis Trollope, *Domestic Manners of the Americans* (London: Oxford University Press, 2014), originally published 1832.

34 *Near the St. James was the fashionable Esplanade Avenue*: City descriptions from maps of nineteenth-century New Orleans at the Library of Congress.

34 *four-thousand-seat auditorium*: *New Orleans Bee*, December 1, 1835, Library of Congress, Charlotte Cushman Papers. Manuscript/Mixed Material.

35 *The walls and ceiling were brightly painted*: Nellie Kroger Smither, *A History of the English Theatre in New Orleans* (New York: B. Blom, 1967).

35 *struggled to fill the cavernous space*: Stebbins, *Charlotte Cushman*, 22.

35 *"The worst Countess we have had the honor of seeing"*: *New Orleans Bee*, December 4, 1835, quoted in Lisa Merrill, *When Romeo Was a Woman: Charlotte Cushman and Her Circle of Female Spectators* (Ann Arbor: University of Michigan Press, 2000), 28.

35 *"Miss Cushman can sing nothing"*: *New Orleans Bee*, April 12, 1836, quoted in ibid., 28.

35 *"bearable"*: Quoted in Joseph Leach, *Bright Particular Star: The Life and Times of Charlotte Cushman* (Boston: Yale University Press, 1970).

35 *Her tone was now "aspirated"*: James Murdoch, *The Stage*, 1880, quoted in *The Cambridge Handbook to American Theatre*, 237.

36 *"Never fell in love with a lord"*: Olive Logan, *Before the Footlights and Behind the Stage* (Philadelphia: Parmlee & Co, 1870), 133.

36 *"I went on with tolerable composure"*: Horace Howard Furness, *A New Variorum Edition of Shakespeare: Vol II, Macbeth* (Philadelphia and London: J. B. Lippincot & Co., 1873), 415–25.

37 *"fair, feminine, nay, perhaps even fragile"*: Ibid.

38 *"pythoness"*: "Miss Cushman as Meg Merrilies," *New York Times,* January 23, 1887. She was called pythonic many times throughout her career.

38　*At night she climbed up to the garret of the house*: Stebbins, *Charlotte Cushman*.

38　*"a couple of begrimed men in shirt-sleeves"*: Logan, *Before the Footlights*, 72.

40　*short, fat, and four-foot-ten-inches tall*: Stebbins, *Charlotte Cushman*, 22–23.

40　*"was almost insane on the subject"*: Maeder, quoted in Price, *A Life of Charlotte Cushman*, 16–17.

41　*"She made the people understand the character that Shakespeare drew"*: Waters, *Charlotte Cushman*, 5.

41　*"the Slaughterhouse"*: Thomas Bogar, *Thomas Hamblin and the Bowery Theatre: The New York Reign of "Blood and Thunder" Melodramas* (New York: Springer, 2017), 3.

chapter four: The Star of the Bowery

43　*"tremendous pop as of a colossal champagne-cork"*: Henry James, *A Small Boy and Others* (New York: Charles Scribner and Sons, 1913), 317.

43　*"like pictures on the wall"*: Firsthand descriptions of rail travel from Ralph Waldo Emerson, Victor Hugo, Gustave Flaubert, quoted in Wolfgang Schivelbusch, *The Railway Journey: The Industrialization and Perception of Time and Space* (Berkeley: University of California Press, 1986), 52–56.

44　*"train-induced fatigue"*: Ibid., 58, quoting *The Lancet*.

44　*"howl like a dog"*: Ibid.

44　*men in dark suits with worried expressions*: Financial panic began at the end of 1836.

45 *"as if he could clutch almost anything in his talons"*: Lydia Marie Child, quoted in Bogar, *Thomas Hamblin*, 83.

45 *charred mass stretching seventeen blocks*: Herbert Asbury, "The Great Fire of 1831," *New Yorker*, July 26, 1930.

45 *Copper roofs poured down themselves*: Eliza Leslie, "Gleanings and Recollections: No 1, The New York Fire," *Parley's Magazine*, January 1838, 30–33.

46 *a pair of gum arabic shoes*: George Templeton Strong, *The Diary of George Templeton Strong: Vol. 1 Young Man in New York 1835–1849* (New York: Macmillan, 1952).

46 *He told her she was exactly what he was looking for*: Bogar, *Thomas Hamblin*, 146–47.

47 *"If a philosopher wishes to observe"*: Lydia Maria Child, *Letters from New York* (New York: C. S. Francis & Co., 1846), 174.

47 *Hamblin had drilled peepholes for police*: Ibid., 175.

47 *when an actor playing a king pretended to fall asleep*: *Morning Courier and New York Enquirer*, November 28, 1832, quoted in Bogar, *Thomas Hamblin*, 100–101.

48 *"amused themselves by throwing pennies"*: Ibid.

48 *"rain of vegetable glory"*: Quoted in Levine, *Highbrow / Lowbrow*, 28.

48 *"Throw not the pearl of Shakespeare's wit before the swine of the bowery pit" went one popular saying*: Washington Irving compared the gallery gods to "animals" and the theatre itself to Noah's Ark.

48 *"Theatre is divided into three and sometimes four classes"*: Quoted in Levine, *Highbrow / Lowbrow*, 43.

49 *"licks the joints, but bites the heart"*: Known as "Lasegue's

Dictum." Ernst-Charles Lasegue, nineteenth-century French physician, 1864.

49 *"ugly beyond average ugliness"*: "Charlotte Cushman," *New York Times*, February 19, 1876.

chapter five: American Genius

51 *"after some important event"*: James Henry Wiggin, "A House and a Name," *The Bostonian* Vol. 1, 1894–95, 92.

52 *"to create is the proof of a Divine presence"*: Quoted in Kenneth S. Sacks, *Understanding Emerson* (Princeton: Princeton University Press, 2003), 29.

53 *The joke was that "more members of both houses"*: Stebbins, *Charlotte Cushman*, 28.

54 *"bull in black silk"*: Charles Godfrey Leland, *Memoirs of Charles Godfrey Leland* (London: William Heinemann, 1894), 101.

54 *"harsh, but harmonious"*: "The Career of Charlotte Cushman," *Harper's Bazaar*, March 18, 1876.

54 *"magnificently attired"*: Quoted in Waters, *Charlotte Cushman*.

54 *"without injuring the harmony of the verse."*: Quoted in Merrill, *When Romeo Was a Woman*, 39.

56 *"My Dear Darling Sister"*: Charlotte Cushman Papers, Library of Congress.

57 *"The ground liquified under me"*: Stebbins, *Charlotte Cushman*.

chapter six: Gypsy Queen

59 *"suffer* bodily *to cure my heart-bleed"*: Ibid.

61 *"catch some inspiration"*: "Charlotte Cushman: Her Debut as Meg Merrilies," Robinson Locke Scrapbook, 139, New York Library for the Performing Arts, Lincoln Center, quoted in Merrill, *When Romeo Was a Woman*, 42.

61 *she heard one gypsy say to another*: Stebbins, *Charlotte Cushman*, 149.

61 *behind him in the darkness he heard a sound*: Ibid.

62 *imagines the character as an emblem of romantic wildness*: John Keats, "Meg Merrilies," 1818, poetryfoundation.org.

62 *Charlotte crept into the gypsy tent*: Mary Anderson, *A Few Memories* (New York: Harper Brothers Publishers, 1896), 37.

62 *"strange, silent spring"*: Ibid.

62 *"If ever the dead come back among the living"*: Daniel Terry, *Guy Mannering, or, the Gypsy's Prophecy* (Boston: Wells and Lily, 1823).

63 *"so wild and piercing, so full of agony"*: "Women Who Have Assayed the Role of Hamlet," *New York Herald*, June 11, 1899.

64 *more time to rush backstage*: Ibid., 152.

64 *she heard a knock*: Quoted in Stebbins, *Charlotte Cushman*, 149.

64 *"How," the artist asked incredulously*: Ibid., 150.

64 *"She seems to identify herself so completely"*: Walt Whitman, "About Acting," *Brooklyn Daily Eagle*, August 4, 1846.

64 *"The Meg Merrilies of Miss Cushman"*: "Miss Charlotte

Cushman's Last Appearance in America," *Prompter*, 1850, from the Brander Matthews Collection, Houghton Theatre Library, Harvard University.

65 *"Unless one does"*: Augustin Daly, *The Life of Augustin Daly* (New York: Macmillan, 1917), 135.

65 *"noble frenzy of eccentric genius"*: "Charlotte Cushman, The Versatilities of a Great Career," *New York Clipper*, nd (likely 1876), clipping from Charlotte Cushman Collection, Library of Congress.

65 *Edmund Simpson, Charlotte's new boss*: Gerald Bordman and Thomas S. Hischak, "Simpson, Edmund," in *The Oxford Companion to American Theatre* (New York: Oxford University Press, 2004), 625.

65 *He had hair that curled up from his brow*: Description from an image in the New York Public Library for the Performing Arts, Billy Rose Collection.

66 *Simpson had been an actor but taken up managing*: James Grant Wilson and John Fiske, "Edmund Simpson," in *Appleton's Cyclopaedia of American Biography* (New York: D. Appleton, 1909).

66 *the African Grove*: Bruce McConachie, *American Theatre in Context: From the Beginnings to 1870*, Ed. Don B. Wilmeth and Christopher Bigsby (Cambridge: Cambridge University Press, 1998), 144–45.

67 *lame in both legs*: F. B. Sanborn, "A Concord Note Book: Ellery Channing and His Table-Talk," *The Critic*, Volume 47 (Berkeley: University of California, 1905).

68 *"I have felt what it is to be defenseless"*: Charlotte Cushman to Park Benjamin, October 13, nd.

chapter seven: Descent into Five Points

69 *"always given to actresses of little or no position"*: Annie Hampton Brewster, "Miss Cushman," *Blackwood's Magazine*, 1878.

70 *"I was at the mercy of the man"*: Ibid.

70 *"a large proportion of those connected with the Stage"*: Quoted in Stephanie Rosa Galipeau, "Victorian Rebellion in Drag: Cushman and Menken Act Out Celebrity," master's thesis, Florida State University, 2003, 32.

70 *"studying that bare skeleton of a part"*: Quoted in Brewster, "Miss Cushman."

71 *around the lake grew a row of slaughterhouses*: Five Points details from Tyler Anbinder, *Five Points: The 19th-Century New York City Neighborhood That Invented Tap Dance, Stole Elections, and Became the World's Most Notorious Slum* (New York: Simon & Schuster, 2001).

72 *"narrow ways, diverging to the left and right"*: Charles Dickens, *American Notes* (London: A. and W. Galignani, 1842), 104.

72 *Middle-class tourists might pay to go "slumming"*: Ted Chamberlain, "Gangs of New York: Fact vs. Fiction," *National Geographic* (online), March 23, 2003.

73 *"hot corn girls"*: Herbert Asbury, *Gangs of New York* (New York: Thunder's Mouth Press, 1998), originally published in 1927.

73 *decorating their mantels with pictures*: Chamberlain, "Gangs of New York."

73 *"every house was a brothel, and every brothel a hell"*: Ibid.

74 *crisscrossed with shortcuts*: Joe Cowell, *Thirty Years Passed*

Among the Players in England and America: Interspersed with Anecdotes and Reminiscences of a Variety of Persons, Directly or Indirectly Connected with the Drama During the Theatrical Life of Joe Cowell, Comedian (New York : Harper & Brothers, 1844), 56.

74 *Charlotte carefully navigated an alley knee deep with filth*: Ibid.

74 *The galleries were draped in a swath of baize*: Ibid.

74 *the Park was the only one considered fashionable*: Trollope, *Domestic Manners*.

75 *The Park had its own infamous "third tier"*: Rosemarie Bank, *Theatre Culture in America 1825–1860* (Cambridge: Cambridge University Press, 1997).

75 *She reaches for him, but he roughly pushes her away*: Details and dialogue from George Almar's stage adaptation of Dickens's *Oliver Twist*, first produced in 1838.

77 *"the most intense acting ever felt on the park boards"*: Walt Whitman, "About Acting," *Brooklyn Eagle*, August 14, 1846.

chapter eight: First Love

80 *Sully threw out his first painting of Charlotte*: Thomas Sully, Diary. New York Public Library Rare Books and Manuscripts Archive.

83 *Inside the front cover*: Charlotte Cushman, Diary, Columbia University Butler Library Rare Books and Manuscripts.

85 *Charlotte thought marriage between men and women was foolish*: Letters between Charlotte Cushman and Helen Hunt Jackson, Colorado College archive.

85 *"bold and impulsive"*: Cushman, Diary.

86 *She paid $100 for the ticket*: Ibid.

88 *"imagination unchecked"*: Cushman, Diary.

88 *"I have always said that time'l show"*: Charlotte Cushman to Mary Eliza Cushman, March 2, 1845, Charlotte Cushman Papers, Library of Congress.

89 *"more wretched"*: Cushman, Diary.

90 *Charlotte had to rush to Sallie's room*: Ibid.

91 *"glaringly beautiful"*: Ibid.

chapter nine: Enemies Abroad

94 *"Whether she means it as a compliment or not"*: Cushman, Diary.

94 *"quite ill-tempered"*: Charlotte Cushman to Mary Eliza Cushman, December 2, 1844, Charlotte Cushman Papers, Library of Congress.

95 *Charlote and Sallie moved into modest rooms in Convent Garden*: "Some Recollections of the Princess Theatre," *Gentleman's Magazine* vol. 262, 69, https://books.google .com/books?id=tkc3AAAAYAAJ&pg=PA69&lpg=P A69&dq=%22charlotte+cushman%22+fell+on +her+knees+london+theatre+manager&source =bl&ots=uoULdvTpnQ&sig=qtKfzvnzrQgN8ISYA NRKfvPvtw8&hl=en&sa=X&ved=0ahUKEwjF1I aBq73cAhVRMawKHYbtB-IQ6AEIOTAD#v=one page&q=%22charlotte%20cushman%22%20fell%20 on%2her%20knees%20london%20theatre%20man ager&f=false.

95 *At the theatre, Maddox invited her into his office*: George Vandenhoff, *Leaves from an Actor's Note-Book* (New York: D. Appleton & Company, 1860), 186–87.

95 *Maddox recognized at once the energy of Lady Macbeth*: Ibid., 213.

96 *"looking very well and is in very good spirits"*: Charles Cushman to Mary Eliza Cushman, London, May 1, 1845, Library of Congress, Charlotte Cushman Papers.

96 *Forrest had made his debut in a female role*: Bordman, *Oxford Companion to American Theatre*, 268–69.

96 *"iron repose, perfect precision of method"*: William Winter, quoted in William Rounesville Alger, *Life of Edwin Forrest, American Tragedian Vol. 2* (New York: J. B. Lippincott & Company, 1877), 651.

97 *"It was something worse than ridiculous"*: "Princess Theatre," *Guardian and the Observer*, February 24, 1845.

98 *"emptiness of ambition"*: Ibid.

98 *One dissenting observer*: Vandenhoff, *Leaves from an Actor's Note-Book*.

98 *"don't like Americans in the newspapers"*: Charlotte Cushman to Mary Eliza Cushman, March 28, 1845, Library of Congress, Charlotte Cushman Papers.

99 *"brilliant and triumphant success"*: Ibid.

100 *"I have not slept for three nights and look like a ghost"*: Charlotte Cushman to Mary Eliza Cushman, April 17, 1845, Library of Congress, Charlotte Cushman Papers.

chapter ten: Lady Romeo

101 *"a mess of dialogue from [Garrick's] own pen"*: "Miss Cushman and Miss S. Cushman," *Observer*, January 4, 1846.

102 *"in no uncertain terms the difficulty"*: Quoted in Lisa Merrill, "Charlotte Cushman," in *Jameson, Cowden Clarke, Kemble, Cushman: Great Shakespeareans*, Ed. Gail Marshall, Volume VII, Chapter 4 (New York: Bloomsbury, 2011), 141.

102 *Macready sent Charlotte a dagger from one of his own performances*: Celia Laquau, "The Macready Dagger," 1892, unpublished manuscript, Folger Shakespeare Library.

103 *"disclosed that ardent, passionate disposition"*: "Haymarket Theatre: The Misses Cushman as Romeo and Juliet," *Scotsman*, January 3, 1846. In the same newspaper is a report that references *Hamlet* in talking about brain disease as one of the worst ailments "flesh is heir to."

103 *"the bend of the knee, slight sneer of the lip"*: Quoted in Merrill, "Charlotte Cushman."

103 *Charlotte was a convincing swordsman*: *New York Daily Tribune*, November 9, 1860.

104 *"The character of Romeo is one which every man of sentiment takes to himself"*: Quoted in Merrill, *When Romeo Was a Woman*.

104 *"the vivifying spark"*: "Haymarket Theatre: The Misses Cushman."

105 *"entered well into the character"*: George Rowell, *Queen Victoria Goes to the Theatre* (London: P. Elek, 1978), 74. Quoted in Merrill, "Charlotte Cushman," as a footnote.

106 *"most remarkable pieces of acting ever witnessed"*: *Pittsburgh Morning Post*, April 22, 1858, 3.

106 *"lovemaking, as practiced by the other sex"*: *Mercury* (Liverpool), January 18, 1847. Quoted in Merrill, "Charlotte Cushman," 155.

106 *Knowles was steeped in Shakespeare*: Robin O. Warren, *Women on Southern Stages 1800–1865: Performance, Gender and Identity in a Golden Age of American Theater* (Jefferson, NC: McFarland, 2016).

107 *Charlotte reminded him of the famous British tragedian*: *Manchester Guardian*, May 20, 1846.

109 *"Charlotte's was a character"*: "The Misses Cushman," *Musical World*, October 10, 1846.

110 *"all in a blaze of enthusiasm"*: Thomas Carlyle and Jane Welsh Carlyle, Brent E. Kisner, ed. *The Carlyle Letters Online [CLO]* (Durham, North Carolina: Duke University Press, 2007–2016).

111 *Charlotte sent a copy of Eliza's poems*: Geraldine Jewsbury to Charlotte Cushman, nd, Library of Congress, Charlotte Cushman Papers. Quoted in Merrill, *When Romeo Was a Woman*, 151.

111 *"If you ever quarrel"*: Ibid.

112 *She searched Charlotte's face*: Eliza Cook, "To Charlotte Cushman: On Seeing Her Play Bianca in Milman's Tragedy of Fazio," in *Poems* (Abingdon, UK: Routledge, 1861). Detail about Eliza growing ill from breakup with Charlotte is quoted in Merrill, *When Romeo Was a Woman*.

112 *"Darling," she wrote to a young actress*: Charlotte Cushman

to "Dearest," Newcastle on Tyne, December 9, 1845, Library of Congress, Charlotte Cushman Papers. Merrill's research points to a woman named Sarah Anderson as the recipient of the letter.

113 *"I ought to answer immediately"*: Charles Dickens to William Charles Macready, June 29, 1848, Morgan Library and Museum, Rare Books and Manuscripts.

113 *"sell her soul"*: Merrill, *When Romeo Was a Woman*, 159.

chapter eleven: The Greatest American Actress

115 *"I have had a very interesting American visitor"*: Quoted in Henry Chorley, *Letters of Mary Russell Mitford* (London: Second Series, RB Bentley, 1872), Vol. 1, 220.

116 *"What a wonderful creature Miss Cushman is"*: Thomas Higginson, *Letters and Journals of Thomas Wentworth Higginson 1846–1906* (New York: Houghton Mifflin Company, 1921).

116 *"Of course the mother [meant] to intimidate me and mine"*: Charlotte Cushman to Benjamin Webster, January 31, nd, Folger Shakespeare Library.

116 *criticizing the "stupid farces"*: Charlotte Cushman to John Perry, October 14, 1847, New York Public Library, MSS Main.

117 *"You seem to have no stars"*: Ibid.

117 *"I purpose coming to America in August next"*: Ibid.

118 *"a clear half the house each night"*: Quoted in Merrill, *Romeo Was a Woman*, 163.

118 *"I forgot to tell you that we met Miss Cushman"*: Elizabeth Barrett Browning to Arabella Barrett, October 22, 1852,

New York Public Library, MSS Main. Quoted in Robert Browning, *Dearest Isa: Robert Browning's Letters to Isa Blagden*, Ed. Eric McAleer (Austin: University of Texas Press, 1951), 26.

119 *"the greatest American Actress"*: *Daily Morning Post* (Pittsburgh), August 10, 1849.

120 *competing performances of* Macbeth: Nigel Cliff, *The Shakespeare Riots: Revenge, Drama and Death in Nineteenth-Century America* (New York: Random House, 2007).

121 *If it was, as some said, a restaging of the Revolutionary War*: Bruce McConachie, quoted in "The Astor Place Riot: Shakespeare as a Flashpoint for Class Conflict in 1849," *Shakespeare and Beyond*, Folger Shakespeare Library, May 9, 2017.

122 *"out on the open prairie"*: "Charlotte Cushman," nd (likely published in 1876 as a reminiscence of her life), New York Public Library for the Performing Arts.

122 *"An it is herself that is coming now be jabers!"*: Ibid. This area is now the site of multi-hundred-megawatt wind farms.

123 *"felt the power of her personal magnetism"*: Ibid.

123 *"as cordially as if it had been dressed in immaculate kid"*: Ibid.

124 *"vague sense of sadness"*: Julia Markus, *Across an Untried Sea: Uncovering Lives Hidden in the Shadow of Convention and Time* (New York: Knopf Doubleday Publishing Group, 2013).

125 *"selfishly sacrificing" Max's happiness to her own*: Charlotte Cushman to "Darling" (Matilda Hays), May 11, 1849. Library of Congress, Charlotte Cushman papers.

125 paraphrasing Leach, *Bright Particular Star*, 241.

125 *"foreign stamp of approbation"*: Foster, *New York by Gaslight*.

126 *"thousand mouths [are] feeding on me"*: Charlotte Cushman to "Darling" (Sarah Anderton,) quoted in Merrill, *When Romeo Was a Woman*, 170.

chapter twelve: Rome

132 *"with more sunbeams"*: Nathaniel Hawthorne to Grace Greenwood [Sarah Jane Clarke Lippincott], April 17, 1852, New York Public Library Digital Collections.

132 *"detestation of pen and ink"*: Nathaniel Hawthorne to Grace Greenwood [Sara Jane Clarke Lippincott], April 17, 1852, New York Public Library Digital Collections.

132 *"After the impression of her own face"*: Ibid.

133 *women in the house liked him so much*: Merrill, *When Romeo Was a Woman*, 173.

133 *"if she has inventive powers as an artist"*: Henry James, *William Wetmore Story and His Friends* (London: William Blackwood, 1903), 257.

133 *her voice sounded savage and too masculine*: Ibid., 255.

134 *one guest felt that anyone who sat down at their "Apician feasts"*: "Charlotte Cushman: An Interesting Reminiscence from Her Life in Rome Twenty Years Ago," nd, New York Public Library for the Performing Arts, Billy Rose Theatre Collection.

135 *"just touching the keys so as to give a background to the picture"*: Ibid.

136 *"I can never suffer so much again"*: Charlotte Cushman to

Emma Crow Cushman, nd, Library of Congress, Charlotte Cushman Papers.

137 *black silk velvet, skillfully embroidered*: Smithsonian Museum of American History, archive of costumes worn by Charlotte Cushman.

138 *It was April 1857*: Recounted by Annie Hampton Brewster in her papers at the Boston Historical Society. Some of this also quoted in Merrill, *When Romeo Was a Woman*, 183.

138 *"like fishwives"*: Ibid.

138 *suing her for more than $2,000*: Approximately $60,000 today.

139 *she became more ladylike*: Merrill, *When Romeo Was a Lady*, 190.

chapter thirteen: The Coming Storm

142 *"Saw Charlotte Cushman and had a stage-struck fit."*: Louisa May Alcott, *Louisa May Alcott: Her Life, Letters and Journals* (Boston, Massachusetts: Roberts Brothers, 1892), 99.

142 *"an actress—not even second rate . . ."*: Daniel J. Watermeier, *American Tragedian: The Life of Edwin Booth* (St. Louis: University of Missouri Press, 2015), 66.

143 *"little sweetheart"*: Ibid., 62.

143 *"peculiar intimacy"*: Adam Badeau, "A Night with the Booths," quoted in Watermeier, *American Tragedian*, 63.

143 *"felt that her fate was to marry him"*: Fanny Seward, Diary, March 11, 1864, William Henry Seward Papers, A.S51, Rare Books, Special Collections and Preservation, River Campus Libraries, University of Rochester.

144 *"never having seen it until then"*: Merrill, *When Romeo Was a Woman*, 206.

144 *"Darling mine, I wish you would burn my letters"*: Charlotte Cushman to Emma Crow, June 20, 1858, Library of Congress, Charlotte Cushman Papers.

146 *"a little Charlotte"*: Emma Crow Cushman to Charlotte Cushman, Library of Congress, Charlotte Cushman Papers.

chapter fourteen: Civil Wars

150 *"Standing beside the flag in front of his marble fireplace"*: Leach, *Bright Particular Star*. (This meeting is correlated by a letter from William Seward to Lincoln in the Library of Congress Lincoln Papers and in a letter from Charlotte Cushman to William Seward in the same collection.)

152 *felt his children's education would not be complete*: Henry Swift to William Winter, October 4, 1906, Folger Shakespeare Library. There are a few problems with Swift's story. Cushman sailed for America in 1861 and again in 1863 but the dates of her travels don't match up with the battles Swift describes. Swift dates this voyage around the battle of Antietam, which was fought in September 1862, and Lee's temporary retreat to Virginia and march into Maryland shortly thereafter. Swift remembered meeting Cushman all his life, and he was eighty-six when he wrote to William Winter. It's possible Swift conflated the battles of the war, or transposed one of his many voyages onto another.

152 *a large, two-story red brick building*: Glyndon Van Deusen,

Notes on Sources

William Henry Seward (Oxford: Oxford University Press, 1967).

153 *hoped to be a writer*: Fanny Seward, Diary, Seward House Collections, Seward Family Papers at the University of Rochester.

153 *"massive brows"*: Ibid.

154 *"with the ease and air of habit"*: Doris Kearns Goodwin, *Team of Rivals: The Political Genius of Abraham Lincoln* (New York: Simon & Schuster Paperbacks, 2006), 610–11.

154 *"so overspread with sadness"*: Ibid., 6.

155 *"I think nothing equals Macbeth"*: James Shapiro, *Shakespeare in America: An Anthology from the Revolution to Now* (New York: Library of America, 2014).

155 *"Lincoln was eager to know"*: Goodwin, *Team of Rivals*, 611–12.

155 *A few days before the performance*: Seward, Diary.

157 *"he saw himself as an avenging Brutus"*: Folger Shakespeare Library podcast *Men of Letters: Shakespeare's Influence on Abraham Lincoln.*

157 *"dare-devil"*: Charlotte Cushman to Emma Crow Cushman, May 6, 1865, Library of Congress, Charlotte Cushman Papers.

158 *A doctor was called to identify the body*: William May to Captain Dudley Knox, "The positive identification of the body of John Wilkes Booth," May 18, 1925, New York University Archives.

159 *"We have heard with mingled emotions of horror and regret"*: Draft by Charlotte Cushman, nd, Library of Congress,

Charlotte Cushman Papers. Published without crediting her in *Memorial Record of the Nation's Tribute to Abraham Lincoln*, Ed. Benjamin Franklin Morris (WH & OH Morrison, 1865).

159 *"worn out broken wrinkled lunatic."*: Charlotte Cushman to Helen Hunt Jackson, July 18, 1869, Helen Hunt Jackson Papers, Colorado College.

159 *Charlotte refused anesthetic*: Reported by the Italian revolutionary Giuseppe Mazzini to a friend, in Giuseppe Mazzini, *Letters to an English Family Vol. I* (Devon, UK: John Lane, 1920), 277.

160 *"Newport is the place to live"*: Charlotte Cushman to Kate Field, April 1865, Boston Historical Society.

160 *After the war, Newport became a destination*: John Sterngass, *First Resorts: Pursuing Pleasure at Saratoga Springs, Newport and Coney Island* (Baltimore and London: Johns Hopkins University Press, 2001).

chapter fifteen: Villa Cushman

164 *"Nursing a nostalgia on the sun-warmed rocks"*: Henry James, "The Sense of Newport," *Harpers*, August 1906.

164 *"my sea and my sunsets"*: Quoted in Alexander Nemerov, *Acting in the Night: Macbeth and the Places of the Civil War* (Oakland, CA: University of California Press, 2010).

165 *"It is cruel and wrong"*: Helen Hunt Jackson to Emily Dickinson, Emily Dickinson Museum, Amherst, circa 1884.

165 *"I don't believe any of our American men"*: Charlotte

Cushman to Helen Hunt Jackson, August 18, 1871, Helen Hunt Jackson Papers, Colorado College.

165 *"the gentlemanly little person"*: Ibid., December 6, 1869.

166 *"immediate present seized, held, grabbed, clutched"*: Ibid., August 18, 1871.

166 *"I won't give up reading"*: Charlotte Cushman obituary, *New York Herald*, February 1, 1876.

166 *"When I wish to be antediluvian"*: James, *William Wetmore Story*, 277.

167 *"see every fibre of thatch on the roof"*: Higginson, *Letters and Journals*, January 1872.

167 *"magician"*: George T. Ferris, March 21, 1874, *Appleton's Journal*, reprinted in Waters, *Charlotte Cushman*, 151.

chapter sixteen: Contrary Winds

171 *"Come auntie"*: Charlotte Cushman Obituary, *Harper's Bazaar*, August 26, 1876.

172 *"profusely ornamented"*: Charlotte Cushman obituary, *Chicago Daily Tribune*, February 24, 1876.

173 *"We find little difference"*: Charlotte Cushman obituary, *New York Times*, February 19, 1876.

173 *"Thus we see that Charlotte Cushman"*: "The Career of Charlotte Cushman," *Harper's Bazaar,* March 18, 1876.

173 *"There was hardly a hearthstone"*: Charlotte Cushman obituary, *New York Times*, February 19, 1876.

174 *"Into a face that every man called ugly"*: "The Career of Charlotte Cushman."

epilogue

175 *"Culture is not a fixed condition"*: Levine, *Highbrow / Lowbrow*.

176 *"neither man-woman nor woman-man"*: Likely paraphrased from Beaumont and Fletcher's play *Love's Cure or the Martial Maid*, about a fierce girl who takes her gentle brother's place as a warrior.

176 *"whether any amount of histrionic art or genius"*: "Charlotte Cushman: Some Notes Concerning Her and Her Appearance in Boston Saturday Evening," *New York Times*, October 8, 1863.

177 *than anywhere else in the world*: From research conducted by the Shakespeare Birthplace Trust.

Selected Bibliography

Alcott, Louisa May. *Louisa May Alcott: Her Life, Letters, and Journals*. Boston: Roberts Brothers, 1892.

Anbinder, Tyler. *Five Points: The Nineteenth-Century New York City Neighborhood That Invented Tap Dance, Stole Elections, and Became the World's Most Notorious Slum*. New York: Simon and Schuster, 2001.

Asbury, Herbert. *The Gangs of New York*. New York: Thunder's Mouth Press, 1998.

Bloom, Arthur W. *Edwin Booth: A Biography and Performance History*. Jefferson, North Carolina: McFarland & Company, Inc., Publishers, 2013.

Bogar, Thomas *Thomas Hamblin and the Bowery Theatre: The New York Reign of "Blood and Thunder" Melodramas*. New York: Springer, 2017.

Bordman, Gerald and Thomas S. Hischak. *Oxford Companion to American Theatre*. New York: Oxford University Press, 2004.

Brasher, Thomas L. *Whitman as Editor of the Brooklyn Daily Eagle*. Detroit: Wayne State University Press, 1970.

Browning, Robert and Edward C. McAleer, ed. *Dearest Isa: Robert Browning's Letters to Isa Blagden*. Austin: University of Texas Press, 1951.

Child, Lydia Maria Francis. *Letters from New York*. New York: C.S. Francis & Co., 1846.

Chorley, Henry, ed. *Letters of Mary Russell Mitford*, 2nd series, Vol. 1. London: R. Bentley and son, 1872.

Cliff, Nigel. *The Shakespeare Riots: Revenge, Drama and Death in Nineteenth-Century America*. New York: Random House, 2007.

Cook, Eliza. *Poems*. Abingdon, UK: Routledge, 1861.

Cowell, Joe. *Thirty Years Pass Among the Players in England and America*. New York : Harper & Brothers, 1844.

De Toqueville, Alexis. *Democracy in America: Complete and Unabridged Volumes I and II*. New York: Random House, 2004.

Dickens, Charles. *American Notes*. London: Chapman & Hall, 1842.

Easley, Alexis, Andrew King, and John Morton, eds. *Researching the Nineteenth-Century Periodical Press: Case Studies*. Abingdon, UK: Taylor & Francis, 2017.

Ellerbee, Genevieve. "Voyage to Italia: Americans in Italy in the Nineteenth Century." Lincoln, Nebraska: Sheldon Museum of Art Catalogues and Publications, 2010.

Emerson, Ralph Waldo. *Journals of Ralph Waldo Emerson*, Vol 4. (Boston: Houghton Mifflin, 1909.

Foster, George C. *New York By Gas-light and Other Urban Sketches*. Berkeley, California: University of California Press, 1990.

Grossman, Barbara Wallace. *A Spectacle of Suffering: Clara*

Morris on the American Stage. Carbondale, Illinois: Southern Illinois Press, 2009.

Grossman, Edwina Booth. *Edwin Booth: Recollections by his Daughter, Edwina Booth Grossman, and Letters to her and to his Friends.* Freeport, New York: Books for Libraries Press, 1894.

Goodwin, Doris Kearns. *Team of Rivals: The Political Genius of Abraham Lincoln.* New York: Simon & Schuster, 2006.

Gura, Philip F. *American Transcendentalism: A History.* New York: Hill and Wang, 2007.

Higginson, Thomas Wentworth, and Mary Potter Thatcher Higginson. *Letters and Journals of Thomas Wentworth Higginson, 1846-1906.* New York: Houghton Mifflin Company, 1921.

James, Henry. *William Wetmore Story and His Friends.* London: William Blackwood, 1903.

Marshall, Gail, ed. *Jameson, Cowden Clarke, Kemble, Cushman: Great Shakespeareans,* Vol. VII. New York: Bloomsbury, 2011.

Leach, Joseph. *Bright Particular Star: The Life and Times of Charlotte Cushman.* Boston: Yale University Press, 1970.

Levine, Lawrence. *Highbrow/Lowbrow: The Emergence of Cultural Hierarchy in America.* Boston: Harvard University Press, 1988.

Logan, Olive. *Before the Footlights and Behind the Stage.* Philadelphia: Parmlee & Co., 1870.

Marcus, Sharon. *The Drama of Celebrity.* Princeton, New Jersey: Princeton University Press, 2019.

Markus, Julia. *Across an Untried Sea: Discovering Hidden Lives in the Shadow of Convention and Time*. New York: Knopf Doubleday Publishing Group, 2013.

Mazzini, Giuseppe. *Mazzini's Letters to an English Family Vol 1*. Devon, UK: John Lane, 1920.

Mason, Jeffrey D. *Melodrama and the Myth of America*. Bloomington and Indianapolis: Indiana University Press, 1993.

McConachie, Bruce, Don B. Wilmeth, ed., and Christopher Bigsby, ed. *American Theatre in Context: From the Beginnings to 1870*. Cambridge, UK: Cambridge University Press, 1998.

Merrill, Lisa. *When Romeo Was a Woman: Charlotte Cushman and Her Circle of Female Spectators*. Ann Arbor, Michigan: University of Michigan Press, 2000.

Nemerov, Alexander. *Acting in the Night: Macbeth and the Places of the Civil War*. Oakland, California: University of California Press, 2010.

Price, William Thompson. *A Life of Charlotte Cushman*. New York: Brentano's, 1894.

Robins, Edward. *Twelve Great Actresses*. New York: G.P. Putnam's Sons, 1900.

Sacks, Kenneth S. *Understanding Emerson*. Princeton: Princeton University Press, 2003.

Sarmiento, Ferdinand L. *Life of Pauline Cushman*. Philadelphia: J. E. Potter, 1865.

Seward, Fanny. *Diary*. Seward House Collections. University of Rochester, Seward Family Papers.

Schivelbusch, Wolfgang *The Railway Journey: The Industrialization and Perception of Time and Space in the Nineteenth Century*. Berkeley: University of California Press, 1986.

Selected Bibliography

Shapiro, James. *Shakespeare in America: An Anthology from the Revolution to Now*. New York: Library of America, 2016.

Smither, Nellie Kroger. *A History of the English Theatre in New Orleans*. New York: B. Blom, 1967.

Stebbins, Emma. *Charlotte Cushman: Her Letters and Memories of Her Life*. Boston: Houghton, Osgood, and Company, 1879.

Sterngass, Jon. *First Resorts: Pursuing Pleasure at Saratoga Springs, Newport, and Coney Island*. Baltimore: Johns Hopkins University Press, 2001.

Strong, George Templeton. *The Diary of George Templeton Strong: Vol 1. Young Man in New York, 1835-1849*. The *American Historical Review*, Vol. 58, Issue 4, July 1953.

Sturge, Joseph *A Visit to the United States in 1841*. London: Hamilton, Adams, 1842.

Quinn, Arthur Hobson. *A History of American Drama: From the Beginning to the Civil War*. New York: Appleton-Century-Crofts, Inc. 1951.

Trollope, Francis. *Domestic Manners of the Americans*. London: Oxford University Press, 2014.

Upham, Charles. *Salem Witchcraft, Volumes I and II*. New York: Frederick Ungar Publishing Co., 1867.

Vandenhoff, George. *Leaves from an Actor's Note-Book*. New York: D. Appleton and Company, 1860.

Van Deusen, Glyndon G. *William Henry Seward*. Oxford, UK: Oxford University Press, 1967.

Vaughan, Alden T. and Virginia Mason Vaughan. *Shakespeare in America*. New York: Oxford University Press, 2012.

Warren, Robin O. *Women on Southern Stages, 1800-1865:*

Performance, Gender and Identity in a Golden Age of American Theater. Jefferson, North Carolina: McFarland & Company, Inc., Publishers, 2016.

Watermeier, Daniel J. *American Tragedian: The Life of Edwin Booth*. St. Louis: University of Missouri Press, 2015.

Waters, Clara Erskine Clement. *Charlotte Cushman*. Boston: James R. Osgood and Company, 1882.

Wilmeth, Don B., and Tice L. Miller, eds. *The Cambridge Guide to American Theatre*. Cambridge, UK: Cambridge University Press, 1996.

Wilson, James Grant and John Fiske. *Appleton's Cyclopaedia of American Biography*. New York: D. Appleton, 1909.

Wolter, Jurgen C. *The Dawning of American Drama: American Dramatic Criticism, 1746–1915*. Westport, Connecticut: Praeger Contributions in Theatre Criticism, 1993.

Image Credits

Index

Index

Index

breeches parts of, 3 (*see also* Hamlet and Romeo *below*)
childhood and adolescence in, 13–19, 169
death of, 169–73
farewell performance of, 1–7
father's abandonment of, 13, 21, 28, 57
as Hamlet, 3, 81–83, 121, 125–26
as Lady Macbeth, 3, 8, 36, 38–40, *39*, 49, 86, 97, 121, 126, 150, 157, 278
as Meg Merrilies in *Guy Mannering*, 60–65, *63*, 73, 95, 121, 126, 174, 178
as Nancy in *Oliver Twist*, 69–77, 121, 174, 178
in New Orleans, 33–35, 38–41
return to Manhattan of, 44–46
rheumatic fever bout of, 49–50
in Rome, 6, 118, 126, 129–40, 145–46, 150–51, 159, 165
as Romeo, 3, 5, 7, 58, 60, 97, 100–107, 111–12, 121, 126, 136, 142, 144–45, 174
siblings of, *see* Cushman, Augustus; Cushman Charles; Cushman, Susan
singing voice of, 29–31, 35
train travel by, 42–44, 77–78, 86, 121–23
understanding of Shakespeare by, 78, 83
walking lady roles of, 59, 65, 66
wife of, *see* Stebbins, Emma
Cushman, Elkanah (Charlotte's father), 11, 13–14, 16–17, 21, 57
Cushman, Emma Crow (Ned's wife), 144–46, 154, 160, 161, 165, 170
Cushman, Mary Eliza Babbit (Charlotte's mother), 11–15, 57–58, 84, 96, 100
in Albany, 51–53
birth of children of, 13–15
boardinghouse run by, 17–19
husband's abandonment of, 17, 21, 28, 57
in London, 112, 113
marriage of, 11–12
in New York City, 50, 58, 66, 67, 69, 70

Cushman, Susan (Charlotte's sister), 51, 66–67, 69, 70, 84, 103, 112
childhood of, 14, 17
as Juliet, 100–2
at Laurence salon, 109
marriage to Merriman of, 57–58, 66, 67
in Newport, 161
remarriage of, 113
son of, *see* Cushman, Charles Edwin "Ned"
Cushman School (Boston), 172

Darwin, Charles, 88
Debt collectors, 17
Democracy in America (Tocqueville), 9
Democratic Party, 149
Desdemona (character in *Othello*), 107
De Staël, Mme. Anna Louise Germaine 87–88
Dickens, Charles, 25, 69–72, 75–77, 113, 124, 174
America criticized by, 93–94
Five Points visited by, 71–72
Dickinson, Emily, 10, 74, 165
Dix, John Adams, 2
Douglas, Stephen A., 149
Douglass, Frederick, 120
Dupin, Amantine Lucile Aurore, *see* George Sand

Ecuador, 160
Egypt, 10
Elizabeth I, Queen, 87
Emerson, Ellen, 27–28
Emerson, Ralph Waldo, 10, 27–28, 51, 52, 77, 169
England, 23, 25, 36, 48, 55, 79, 108, 115–19, 124, 126, 151
touring in, 113
Victorian, 119
voyage to, 87–91, 93–94
See also London *and other municipalities*
Erie
Canal (New York State), 52

Fagin (character in *Oliver Twist*), 75
Fastnet Rock (Ireland), 91

Index

Index

Index

Index

Index

About the Author

Tana Wocjzuk is an editor at *Guernica* and teaches at New York University, where she has been a Global Research Initiative fellow. She has written for the *New York Times*, *Tin House*, *BOMB*, *The Believer*, *Vice*, and elsewhere. Wojczuk holds an MFA from Columbia University. She was a finalist for the Gulf Coast Prize in Nonfiction and a poetry fellow at the Helene Wurlitzer Foundation and the Tin House Summer Workshop. Originally from Boulder, Colorado, she lives in Brooklyn, New York.